Rossendale Tr

A Centenary Celebration
1907 – 2007

Harry Postlethwaite

LAYOUT AND COMPUTER ORIGINATION BY JOHN A SENIOR

Below: a classic Leyland-bodied PD2 from the Rawtenstall fleet but carrying the Rossendale fleet name after amalgamation *(Gl)*

Facing page: an equally classic East Lancashire-bodied PD2 No. 5 in the Haslingden fleet showing the traditional blue livery which was lost on amalgamation. *(GL)*

Introduction

The Borough of Rossendale, situated in the east of the County of Lancashire, comprises the Forest of Rossendale, not an area of intensive woodland but an area of wild open moorland, and situated to the north of the steep sided Rossendale Valley, through which flows the River Irwell. The main townships, situated in the valley and working from west to east are Haslingden, Rawtenstall and Bacup, all of which are quite small. The Borough provides something of an oasis situated as it is in an area dominated by larger towns, which were, in the past, the home to heavy industry, particularly related to the cotton trade. To the north there are the larger towns of Blackburn, Accrington and Burnley and to the south the towns of Bolton, Bury and Rochdale all of which have been involved, to a greater or lesser extent, in the provision of transport to the Rossendale Valley. In the early days the Rossendale area was involved in the cotton industry, particularly in connection with bleaching and dyeing, but the main industry in more recent times has been footwear, although this has now reduced to the point where manufacturing, once the bedrock of activity in the Valley, is virtually extinct.

Historically, both Haslingden and Rawtenstall Corporations had their own transport undertakings but Bacup never operated vehicles of any kind, despite owning the tramway infrastructure within its boundaries. To the south, part of the present Borough of Rossendale was formerly part of Ramsbottom Urban District Council, which operated its own trolleybuses and buses.

To oversee the various municipal activities in the early 20th century, responsibility for representing the interests of the local community was vested in various committees, composed of elected councillors and appointed officers. The Transport Committee was one such function and separate committees ran their own transport departments in each of the separate municipalities.

As the 20th century progressed, it became apparent that economies of scale could be made, initially by sharing a General Manager between the smaller undertakings and later, by merging them to form joint committees with elected representatives from the constituent authorities.

The formation of Rossendale Joint Transport Committee in 1968 presaged the Local Government reorganisation of 1974 when the Borough of Rossendale was formed from the previous corporations of Haslingden, Rawtenstall and Bacup together with parts of neighbouring areas, notably Whitworth and the Edenfield and

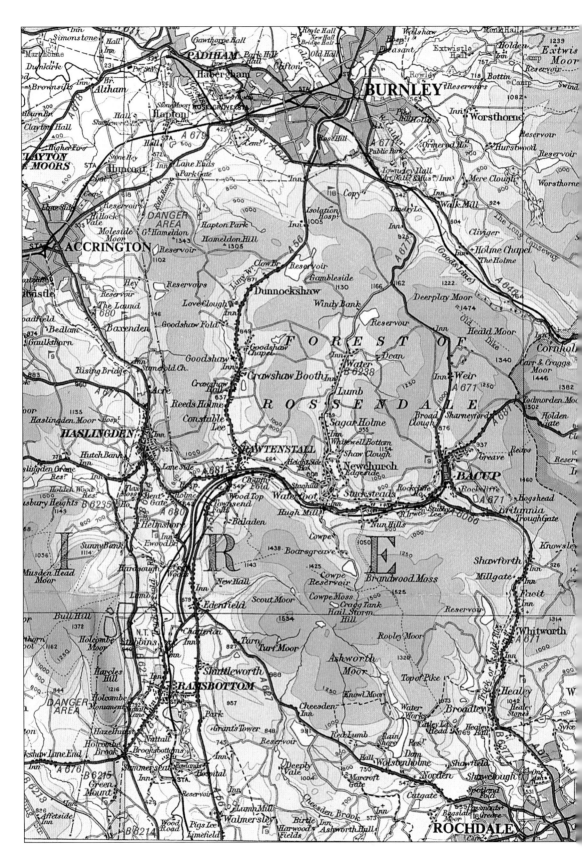

4

Stubbins area of the former Ramsbottom UDC.

This reorganisation resulted in the relatively recently created Joint Transport Committee becoming Rossendale Borough Transport under the auspices of the newly created Rossendale Borough Council.

It could have been a different story had the original Local Government reorganisation proposals been implemented, for that would have meant that parts of the present Borough of Rossendale would have been subsumed into adjoining areas such as Bury, Rochdale and Hyndburn. The outcry from local residents was vociferous and fortuitously, as it turned out, Rossendale Borough Transport was formed into a separate organisation and not combined into a larger undertaking with adjoining Hyndburn.

In 1969, Whitworth, parts of Bacup south towards Rochdale and the whole of the Urban District of Ramsbottom, including Stubbins and Ramsbottom, were included in the South East Lancashire and North East Cheshire Passenger Transport Authority (SELNEC) and so from that date, the Ramsbottom bus operations passed to SELNEC.

Whilst 1974 saw Whitworth, Stubbins and Edenfield incorporated into the new Rossendale area, the former SELNEC boundaries of 1968 are still recognised to this day for validity of GMPTE concessionary passes and the System One Travelcard scheme.

Further political upheaval was to follow eleven years later with the publication of the Transport Act 1985, the intention of which was to deregulate the passenger transport industry and encourage competition from new operators. The legislation required local authorities to create separate 'arms-length' limited companies; accordingly, in 1986, Rossendale Transport Limited was formed with the Borough Council as the sole shareholder.

It is somewhat ironic that the larger towns previously mentioned all had their own municipal transport undertakings, which have either been absorbed into the Greater Manchester Passenger Transport Executive Area or sold to larger private transport operators. Not only does Rossendale Transport now provide local services in some of these towns, it is now the last municipally owned bus company in East Lancashire.

Interestingly, it was Rawtenstall Corporation that received the first production Leyland PD2 double-decker whilst Ramsbottom took the last traditional front-engined double-decker, a Leyland PD3, to be delivered in the United Kingdom. Happily, the latter survives in preservation, keeping alive the memory of locally-owned transport.

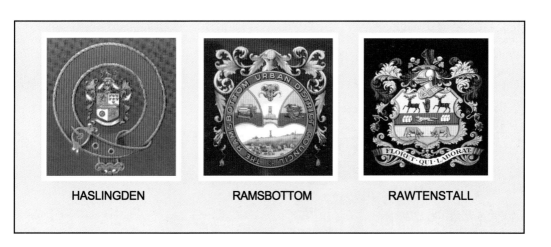

HASLINGDEN   RAMSBOTTOM   RAWTENSTALL

Facing page: A map from the mid-1960s showing the area covered by the three municipalities, and, later, the extension of operations to Rochdale. Manchester is to the south, of course. The brown areas indicating the high ground clearly define the steep and hilly nature of the area. *(STA/PF)*

The Early Days of Transport

Like many other areas, public transport in the Rossendale area commenced with horse-drawn buses or coaches, later to be followed by tramway systems.

As early as 1824 there was a horse-drawn coach service named 'The Traveller' operating from Manchester to Clitheroe via Bury, Haslingden and Accrington. It operated daily except Fridays, travelling out to Clitheroe in the mornings and returning the same evening. A wagonette named 'The Princess Alice' owned by the proprietor of the Commercial Hotel, Haslingden, operated a service between Baxenden and Rawtenstall via Haslingden prior to the opening of the steam tramway service.

Another early operator was William Roberts of the White Horse Hotel, Rawtenstall, who began operation in 1864. His Rossendale Division Carriage Company commenced a service to Rochdale and later operated services from Rawtenstall to Haslingden, Water and Burnley, later trading as W Roberts and Company Limited with stables adjacent to the Bishop Blaize Hotel in Rawtenstall. He stabled up to 20 horses here but with the arrival of steam trams he progressed to motor buses and was succeeded in the business by his son John. He commenced with three motor buses, two of them Darraqs with which two Frenchmen came, and the other a Critchley Norris which became quite famous in its day. It was driven by Mr McWicker of Bacup and was later purchased by Todmorden Corporation as their first motor bus and operated a service between Todmorden and Bacup. Continued operation of motor buses became impossible due to the refusal of the local authorities to grant operating licences.

Two tramway companies, both steam operated, contributed to the establishment of public transport in Rossendale. The Accrington Steam Tramways Company operating under the Accrington Corporation Tramways Act 1882 commenced operation from Accrington Market Place to Baxenden Station on 12th June 1886 and extended this on 27th August 1887 to the Commercial Hotel in the centre of Haslingden. The trams were known as 'The Baltic Fleet'.

There was a further extension on 10th November 1887 to Queens Square, Rawtenstall, by the Queens Arms Hotel. The journey to Accrington took 30 minutes and the single fare was 4d. The length of track within Haslingden, a total of 2.9 miles, was owned by Haslingden Corporation and leased to the Tramway Company. The system commenced using nine Thomas Green tram locos and ten enclosed double-deck trailers manufactured by Falcon, further details of which together with subsequent additional stock are given in the fleet summary in the pictorial section.

The origins of The Rossendale Valley Tramways Company came from the ambitious plans of the Manchester, Bury, Rochdale and Oldham Steam Tramways Company. The Manchester, Bury and Rochdale Tramways (Extension) Order 1882 had authorised a line from Rochdale to Bacup and then westwards to Rawtenstall. It was agreed that the

A horse-drawn bus of Rossendale Carriage Co – Roberts & Co – on service between Rawtenstall & Burnley in 1899 with its driver Bill Collinge. The company also operated to Rochdale. *(RLIB)*

A view in the Thrutch around 1900 with a Rossendale Valley steam tram approaching Waterfoot. Note the enclosed double-deck trailer, necessary to keep cinders emitted by the engine from landing amongst the passengers. *(RLIB)*

section from Facit to Rawtenstall should form a separate undertaking named The Rossendale Valley Steam Tramways Company.

The Rossendale Tramways Act 1888 enabled The Rossendale Steam Tramways Company to take over the authorised tramway, changed the gauge to 4ft 0ins and authorised through running with the Accrington Corporation Steam Tramways Company. The tramways involved the section from Bacup through the Rossendale Valley to Queens Square, Rawtenstall and from Queens Square to Holmfield. Work commenced in September 1888 and about 150 men worked on the scheme with Mr Love as the Resident Engineer. The contractor was Contract Construction Company and at a General Meeting of RVT it was reported that construction costs were £5,280 per mile of single track tramway, £800 per engine and £240 per tramcar.

On Friday 25th January 1889 a formal inspection was carried out by Maj Gen Hutchinson of the Board of Trade, covering the section from Queens Square to Waterfoot. The following day a dinner was held at the Queens Hotel attended by about 30 guests and directors. These included Mr Greene, Vice Chairman, Mr Thomas, Assistant Engineer, Mr Love (Jnr), Manager, Mr Whitmore, Depot Foreman, Mr Forrest, Foreman at the Road, and Mr Love (Snr), Director. Engines were supplied by Thomas Green and tramcars by G F Milnes, Birkenhead and a depot was built in Bacup Road, Rawtenstall. Operations commenced on Thursday 31st January 1889 from Rawtenstall to Waterfoot but there was no through running with Accrington Steam Tramways Company, despite the fact that the tracks were of the same gauge and connected

at Queens Square. Had this through facility been provided, it would have made possible the longest steam tramway journey in the country from Whitewell, Darwen to Waterfoot and later to Bacup. It is reported, however, that on the occasion of the closure of steam tramways in Darwen, in June 1900, a civic party travelled by steam tram from Darwen to Bacup. The 40 strong party left Bull Hill, Darwen at 11am and rode to Bacup in the same car. They travelled via Darwen, Blackburn, Oswaldtwistle, Church, Accrington, Haslingden, Rawtenstall and the Rossendale Valley. The difficulty at Blackburn was overcome by the car being backed into St Peter Street and then continuing along Jubilee Street. At Accrington a lunch stop was made at the Commercial Hotel where Alderman Lee (Accrington) presided with Alderman Oddie (Blackburn) as vice president. Various toasts were offered and following a photograph, the party departed at 3.30pm, arriving in Bacup just before 5pm, having covered 21 miles. As far as can be established, this was the only occasion when such a journey was made.

In May 1889, construction work commenced on the section between Waterfoot and Bacup whilst in the following month, work began on the line to Holmfield. Both sections were inspected by the Board of Trade on Thursday 25th July 1889 and the certificate arrived on Saturday 3rd August 1889, enabling services to commence to Bacup later that day, the first tram arriving in Bacup at 1pm. On Thursday 8th August 1889, operations commenced between Queens Square and Holmfield. The rolling stock comprised nine steam locomotives and ten tramcars. Extension of the tramway from Holmfield to Crawshawbooth commenced in April 1891 and was inspected by the Board of Trade on Wednesday 9th September 1891 with operations starting on Saturday 12th September 1891.

On 10th January 1896, the Manager, Mr William Love, was killed at Waterfoot when he fell from a tramcar, sustaining serious injuries from which he died about one hour later. At the inquest, a verdict of accidental death was recorded. Mr William North, formerly chief engineer, was subsequently appointed manager.

The first conductor on the steam trams was Mr Dennis Hegarty, who later became Markets Inspector for Rawtenstall, a position from which he retired in July 1943. A driver who had early connections with the steam trams was Mr Albert Incles, who recalled driving the first steam tram when the section to Crawshawbooth was opened. He also recalled driving the retained steam engine as a snow plough and being called out in the middle of many nights to clear the tracks for the electric trams.

In July 1898 a half share in the company was acquired by British Electric Traction who planned to electrify the system, but disagreement between Bacup and Rawtenstall Councils caused delay until the 21 year lease on the tramway system had almost expired. Later, the Rossendale Valley Tramways Act 1902 gave powers for electrification and was unopposed by Bacup and Rawtenstall Councils. The system was then purchased jointly by both councils on 1st October 1908 with Rawtenstall operating the system. The operation of steam trams continued until 22nd July 1909, by which time it was the last example of regular steam traction on a street tramway in Britain. Further information on the development of the tramway under Corporation ownership is given in the section on 'Rawtenstall Corporation Transport'.

Whilst many were no doubt happy to see the passing of the steam tram, this was by no means universal and the following letter dated 20th January 1922 was sent by Mr RH Coe of Accrington to the editor of Locomotion News and Railway Contractor, appearing in the issue dated 25th February 1922 and headed 'Old Steam Tram Engines'

'Sir, *It might interest some of your readers to know that the East Lancashire towns of Haslingden and Rawtenstall each still preserve an old steam tram engine, which they use for the purpose of keeping the electric tramways clear during heavy snowfalls. The Haslingden engine is No.1 of the now defunct Accrington and District Steam Tramways Company. It was built by Green and Co. of Leeds in 1887 and is an 0-4-0 well-tank completely enclosed, of course, for working through the streets. The Rawtenstall machine is No. 8 of the old Rossendale Valley Tramways, now owned by Rawtenstall Corporation and was also built by Green and Co. in 1887. During the recent heavy snowfall, which, even for East Lancashire, was a record one, these two fine old locomotives kept their respective tramway systems open, when many other tramway systems in the district were entirely blocked, which thus once more demonstrates the superiority of steam over electricity?'*

The author, as an electrical engineer, refrains from comment on this last line!

A charabanc outside *The Volunteers Hotel,* Turnpike, Newchurch on Friday 16th May 1913, and about to depart on a trip to London, returning on Sunday 18th. It must have been something of an endurance test to undertake such a journey in a vehicle of this type. The driver, wisely, has placed two stones to act as scotches under the rear wheels, thus preventing an accidental runaway. EN 344 was apparently owned by Bury corporation whose coat of arms appears on the side. *(RLIB)*

Ramsbottom Urban District Council

Ramsbottom is a small town north of Bury, and whilst the town itself now forms part of Bury Metropolitan Borough, the villages of Edenfield and Stubbins, which were formerly part of a larger Urban District of Ramsbottom, now form part of the Borough of Rossendale. It always had close associations with Haslingden and Rawtenstall and became the only Urban District Council in Lancashire to operate a transport undertaking into the postwar period. It all started in 1903 when, after a period of consideration, it was decided to seek powers for the construction of a tramway. The powers were granted under the 1903 Tramways Act but it was soon realised that the requirements of the Act were quite onerous. The creation of the tramway was going to involve the rebuilding of a bridge, the reconstruction of a road and the removal of a level crossing.

These requirements, when taken together, were clearly going to impose a financial burden on a small authority, burdens which the council could not justify.

There had been an earlier proposal, put forward by the Lancashire Light Railway Company, to construct a tram line from Blackburn to Manchester via Rawtenstall and Ramsbottom which would have operated under the grand name of the 'Turton, Tottington, Ramsbottom and Rawtenstall Light Railway', but this failed to materialise. An approach was made to Bury Corporation to see if it would be willing to extend existing lines to form a loop through Ramsbottom but after much discussion this also failed to materialise. As a consequence of this it was decided to abandon the idea of a tramway and consider the operation of railless traction, ie trolleybuses. At a Council meeting on 12th January 1912 it was agreed to promote a Bill to authorise the operation of trolleybuses over the roads previously included in the Tramway Act which had been due to expire in August 1912 if the works covered by it were not completed. This Bill received Royal Assent on 25th June 1912 as the Ramsbottom Urban District Council Railless Traction Act, and authorised the operation of trolleybuses on the routes previously covered by

Ramsbottom's first trolleybus, No.1, taken on 14th August 1913 when operation began. It is a Railless with bodywork by Milnes Voss. *(RLIB)*

the Tramways Act. The Act included a provision that the trolleybuses could be replaced at a later date by trams.

The initial route was from the Railway Station at Holcombe Brook on the Lancashire and Yorkshire Railway line, along Bolton Road West, Bolton Street, Market Place, Ramsbottom Lane, Stubbins Lane, Bolton Road North, Bury Road and Market Street to the terminus at Edenfield. Also included was a short spur along Bridge Street to Ramsbottom Station although this section was discontinued from October 1914.

An order for four trolleybuses was placed with the Railless Traction Company Limited, the chassis being supplied to the Railless Company by David Brown of Huddersfield. Each bus was powered by two 20HP motors controlled by tram style hand controllers. The rear entrance open platform bodies were supplied by Milnes Voss, and the first bus was delivered on Sunday 10th August 1913 having been towed from Leeds. A trial run was organised for the following morning and on Thursday 14th August 1913 a Board of Trade inspection of the system took place and the line was approved for operation. On the same evening at 6pm trolleybus No.1 was brought out of the depot to commence operation, news of which soon spread with the result that there were many passengers and also crowds of roadside onlookers. The second trolleybus arrived the following day and by the end of the next week the remaining two trolleybuses arrived to complete the order.

The combination of solid tyres and the granite setts of the roads in the area had an adverse effect on the structure of the bodies and within two years they were in need of replacement. To facilitate this, a further two trolleybuses were ordered from the Railless Traction Company but these were fitted with bodies by Lockwood and Clarkson who then received an order to rebody the original four trolleybuses, a process which took place over the next few years. In 1922 a further trolleybus was purchased, having been ordered from the Railless Company, but built by Thornycroft with body by Short Brothers. Further rebuilding of the trolleybuses was required by 1923 and this was undertaken by the Railless Company. Not only did the solid tyres and setts have an effect on the vehicle bodies but also on the bodies of passengers. One man remarked, 60 years later, "You used to step off them and your body would be shaking".

The first motor bus route was begun in the middle of 1923 with a service from the trolleybus terminus at Edenfield to Rawtenstall Railway Station and operated by two Thornycroft buses numbered 9 and 10. It was reported in August 1924 that Ramsbottom Urban District Council had rejected the offer put forward by Rawtenstall Council for the takeover of Ramsbottom's motor bus services. However, the route and the two vehicles were taken over by Rawtenstall Corporation on 1st September 1924, subsequently being extended to Bury and connected to the Rawtenstall to Burnley Summit service to provide a through facility between Bury and Summit. From 21st November 1924 the service was operated jointly by Bury, Ramsbottom and Rawtenstall.

By October 1924 Ramsbottom Council decided to abandon the trolleybus service which, by then, was only operating for part of the day with motor buses being used for the remainder of the day. To facilitate this, a Parliamentary Bill was promoted to obtain wider powers for the operation of motor buses and this was subsequently passed as the Ramsbottom UDC Act 1926.

A new service was started, from 18th November 1926, between Bury and Rawtenstall via Holcombe Brook and Ramsbottom operated jointly with Bury and Rawtenstall Corporations, part of which coincided with the trolleybus service with the result that trolleybuses made only rare appearances. Officially, all trolleybuses had been withdrawn by 1928, but it was 31st March 1931 when the last trolleybus operated, an event which passed without ceremony.

Whilst a total of nine Thornycroft buses had been purchased in the years 1922 to 1926, buses of Leyland manufacture first entered the fleet in 1927 when three Leyland Lion single-deckers were purchased. Thereafter, all vehicles purchased new were of Leyland manufacture.

On 31st March 1932 the joint service between Bury and Burnley Summit was withdrawn on instructions from the newly-created Traffic Commissioners and replaced by a service between Bury and Rawtenstall, and whilst Ramsbottom remained a joint operator, the service was then worked by Bury and Rawtenstall Corporations. Ramsbottom operated the service via Holcombe Brook together with short workings and local services to Edenfield via Shuttleworth and to Holcombe village, services which continued, albeit

Number 18, a 1928 Leyland PLSC3 Lion with Leyland body had an unfortunate accident whilst descending Bury Road into Rawtenstall. Recovering a vehicle from a predicament such as this would not be easy. *(RMC)*

During World War 2 this Roe-bodied Lion was used as a mobile recruiting office for the RAF. The card shown here, which was sent to local organisations, was signed by the Chairman of the Transport Committee. *(STA)*

with changes in frequency, throughout the life of the undertaking.

Ramsbottom did not acquire any double-deck buses until 1947 when six Leyland PD2/1 models with Leyland bodywork were purchased. The problem in the past had been the low railway bridge at Stubbins but the lowering of the road under the bridge allowed double-deckers to be used. Whilst this solved the problem regarding the use of double-deckers it has been said that it increased the risk of flooding at this point.

With effect from April 1951, Ramsbottom agreed that the General Manager of the Haslingden and Rawtenstall undertakings should, in addition, be appointed as General Manager of Ramsbottom.

The early 1950s saw the purchase of four Royal Tigers, of which the three Roe-bodied vehicles later passed to Rawtenstall (1) and Haslingden (the other pair). A solitary all-Leyland PD2 also joined the fleet, but there were no more purchases until 1961 when fleet numbering reverted to number 1 with the first of nine double-deckers which were delivered in the period up to 1967.

Another acquisition in 1967 was an Albion Nimbus small capacity single-decker with 31 seat body by Weymann, which was purchased from

Warrington Corporation. This bus, originally new to Halifax Corporation, was required to enable one-man conversion of the Holcombe Village service which had to turn in the car park of a local pub.

Preferring to remain independent, Ramsbottom declined to join the Joint Transport Committee set up between Haslingden and Rawtenstall Corporations in 1968 but ironically, later in 1968 the formation of the South East Lancashire and North East Cheshire Passenger Transport Executive was announced. This new body was to take control of all public transport within the Greater Manchester area which included the Urban District of Ramsbottom. Ramsbottom, being very much on the fringe of this area, objected strongly to this proposal, which meant the loss of its own transport undertaking and voiced its objection to the Ministry of Transport. A public meeting was held attended by more than 200 people who pledged their support to the council and a motion that their MP Mr Anthony Greenwood should be instructed to give his support to the objection was carried unanimously. However, it was all to no avail and Ramsbottom became part of SELNEC with effect from November 1969.

Ramsbottom's final vehicle order was for two East Lancashire Coachbuilders-bodied Leyland PD3s, the second of which had the distinction of being the last conventional front-engined double-decker to enter service in Great Britain, although,

Still giving good service in Bury in April 1949 is No. 8, a 1937 Leyland TS7 with its handsome original Roe bodywork. Note the overhead wires; Bury's trams had finished only a few weeks earlier on 13th February 1949. (RM)

sadly this was delivered direct to SELNEC, a few weeks after the demise of Ramsbottom's own transport undertaking.

A well-known character on Ramsbottom buses retired in August 1969 after 20 years' service. She was clippie Mrs Florence Hilton better known to passengers as Florrie who served on the buses from March 1941 to May 1946 and from March 1948 until her retirement. She was known for her cheerful disposition and tribute was paid to her at the July 1969 meeting of Ramsbottom's Finance and General Purposes Committee, which was summed up by Councillor Terrence Fellows with the words, 'She has given valuable service'. Her husband Harold was a driver with the undertaking from November 1945.

Whilst the town of Ramsbottom transferred into Greater Manchester as part of the 1974 Local Government reorganisation, residents of the villages of Stubbins and Edenfield, previously part of Ramsbottom Urban District Council, became part of the new Borough of Rossendale. If only this logic had been followed in 1968, then perhaps Ramsbottom's buses would also have become part of Rossendale Transport.

Haslingden Corporation Transport

Under the Haslingden Corporation Act of 1906, powers were granted to the Borough to construct three branch lines to Helmshore, Ewood Bridge and to the Cemetery on Grane Road. The Act also included powers to operate motor bus services and the Council decided that these would be more suited to the routes in question. Arising from this, the Transport Committee arranged for a demonstration by a double-deck omnibus on 19th January 1907. This turned out to be something of a disaster as foul weather resulted in the bus being very difficult to handle and following two near disasters on the descent into Blackburn most of the civic party made their way on foot to the lunch stop. The return journey was no better with the bus almost overturning on the parapet of the Cock Bridge between Whalley and Great Harwood. On arrival at the Clayton-le-Moors tram terminus, some passengers took the opportunity of returning home on the steam trams. Some reports indicate that this bus was a Ryknield but other reports indicate that eleven days *after* this trial, the Ryknield agent arrived in Haslingden with a double-deck bus and offered a trial run over the route of the previous trial. His offer was declined, hardly surprisingly.

However, the Committee later agreed to the purchase of a Leyland X type single-deck bus and this commenced operation on 12th November 1907 on the proposed tram route to Helmshore. The vehicle, which was registered B 2113, is thought to have carried a red livery. On the previous day a trial trip was arranged to Southport but several of the councillors who had been on the previous trial trip announced that 'they had other business on that day'. A councillor who had not been on that trip turned up with a good supply of sticking plaster! Before the start, travellers gathered at the Municipal Offices saw in the grounds, a large stone with a card attached which read :

> **'WARNING**
> To passers by who wonder what I'm here for,
> Don't laugh or jeer; just shed a silent tear, for
> Know that once I stood at Cock Bridge, Whalley,
> Now here I lie, a monument to folly.'

On the opening day over 400 passengers were carried with as many as 45 being on the 23-seat bus at one time. The single fare was 2d and there

Haslingden's first bus was this Leyland X model with Leyland bodywork dating from 1907. Note the solid tyres, with twins at the rear, and the bench seat allowing passengers to sit with the driver. *(RMC)*

was a 1d stage to Flaxmoss. It was reported in the Rossendale Free Press that the bus had 'manifested consistently good behaviour and has been in gratifying demand'. Despite this flourishing start, the service was not considered to be a success and was withdrawn on 24th July 1909 when the bus was converted to a tower wagon. It was to be some time before there were any further attempts to operate a bus service.

In 1907 Accrington Corporation had purchased the track and rolling stock of the Steam Tramways Company with the intention of carrying out electrification. This electrification was completed as far as Baxenden Station and operation from Accrington to this point commenced on 1st January 1908. On this same date Haslingden Corporation purchased eight Thomas Green locos and eight trailer cars from the Steam Tramways Company to enable it to continue the service through Haslingden. The trams were operated by Accrington on behalf of Haslingden.

Electrification in Haslingden commenced on the last Monday in March 1908 starting at the Baxenden end of the line. The Mayor, Alderman Hamilton, together with the Chairman of the Electricity and Tramways Committee, Alderman Barlow, the Chairman of the General Works Committee, Alderman Cartin, and the Borough Surveyor, Mr J S Green, attended. The Mayor and the Chairman of the Tramways and Electricity Committee both had a hand in the loosening of the old setts watched by about 50 navvies who were looking for work. The electric tram service commenced to the Commercial Hotel on 5th September 1908, four days after a Board of Trade inspection of the track. A decorated tram was driven by the Mayor, Alderman Hamilton, and was greeted by a large crowd in the town centre. The extension to the Rawtenstall Borough boundary at Lockgate opened on 20th October 1908. One steam tram was retained as a snow plough but the remainder were disposed of. An agreement was reached with Accrington Corporation whereby Accrington trams operated the section within Haslingden with Haslingden paying a fee to Accrington and also paying for the electricity used. Haslingden Corporation provided its own tramway inspectors. It was reported in April 1909 that Accrington Electricity Committee had accepted a tender from Brush Electrical Engineering Company for the supply of two double-deck and one single-deck tramcars for this purpose.

At a meeting of Haslingden Town Council in May 1909 approval was given to a proposal by the Tramways Committee to erect tramway offices at a cost of £450.

Map of Haslingden Tramways and Connections.

Haslingden found itself in a strategic position between Accrington and Bacup and although it constructed and leased the tramlines it was only ever an operator of steam trams, and then for a very short period; electric trams ran over the lines from Accrington and Ratwtenstall. *(RLIB)*

At noon on 1st May 1930 the engine of Haslingden bus No.7 is started – by the handle – to mark the replacement of the trams, whilst a stray dog at the left of the photograph seems to be wondering what all the fuss is about. If the petrol engine backfires, as they often did, he will be in for a rude awakening.   *(HL)*

Subsequently, through operation of the tramway between Accrington and Bacup was achieved, and details leading up to this are given under the Rawtenstall Corporation Transport chapter.

The Transport Committee authorised the building of a depot in John Street and four of the Accrington trams were housed there at a cost to Accrington of £50 per year. This Agreement was terminated in 1916 when Accrington discovered that a local haulier was renting space in the depot and storing waste paper, which Accrington considered to be potentially dangerous.

Omnibus operations to Helmshore were resumed in 1919 with the purchase of a BSA light van which was converted to a 12 seater bus by a local wheelwright, Heap and Son of Clegg Street, Haslingden. It was built with a front entrance for one-man operation and was known as 'The Whippet'. However, it proved unreliable and was replaced the following year by an Austin with body by Barnes and Son, Private Lane, Helmshore, also designed for one-man operation. It is thought that Haslingden was a pioneer of one-man operation of buses. In the following years other routes were tried but none was successful. Fleet numbering was introduced with the purchase of Guy single-deckers, numbered 1 and 2, which appeared in 1924 and 1925 respectively.

An express bus service which duplicated the Accrington to Bacup tram service was commenced in 1928 and this connected at Bacup with the network of express services in the Greater Manchester area, initiated by Manchester Corporation.

To operate this service, two Leyland single-deckers, numbered 3 and 4, were purchased in 1928 and 1929. All subsequent purchases, except those during the wartime 'utility' period, were to be vehicles from this manufacturer.

The decision to abandon trams was made in 1929, Haslingden being the first town in the area to reach such a decision. For the conversion, Haslingden purchased 6 Leyland LT1 single-deckers, numbered 5-10. This was the largest order for buses ever placed by Haslingden and increased the fleet from four to ten. The last tram operated on 1st May 1930 and Captain Baxter, Chairman of the Transport Committee, started bus number 7 and then drove this to Accrington. It has been reported that the abandonment of the trams was welcomed by wireless enthusiasts along the route who had suffered from interference caused by the trams. Following this, the express bus service became a stage carriage service operated jointly by the three corporations of Accrington, Haslingden and Rawtenstall. The bus service operated on a 10 minute headway which was increased to 5 minutes at rush hour and on Saturday

Haslingden's first post-war single-deckers, numbered 1-4, comprised two Leyland PS1 and two PS2 models, delivered in 1949. All four had bodies by HV Burlingham of Blackpool, and No. 2 is shown in Haslingden in June 1951. This bus has been preserved in Haslingden livery and often appears at rallies.
(RM)

afternoons. The service became Accrington service No. 4 but the other operators did not use service numbers.

Two more Leyland single-deckers, numbered 11 and 12, arrived in 1931 but 1932 saw the first double-decker purchases, comprising two Leyland TD2s with Leyland bodies, numbered 14 and 15, there being no number 13; this was not used until 1957. Six more Leyland double-decks were purchased during the 1930s and enabled the withdrawal of the first four single-decks.

During the Second World War when there were restrictions on the purchase of new buses, the Corporation took delivery of three double-deckers, a Guy Arab with Northern Counties body numbered 22 in 1942, a Daimler CWG6 with Brush body numbered 23 in 1943 and a Daimler CWA6 with Brush body numbered 24 in 1945, all to the wartime utility specification. The first two had lowbridge bodies and the other a highbridge body. In those days operators did not have a choice of chassis or body manufacturer but had to accept what was allocated to them.

Following the cessation of hostilities, and the lifting of restrictions on the purchase of new vehicles, fleet renewal commenced in 1946 with a return to Leyland Motors as supplier and the delivery of a PD1 double-decker, numbered 25, with a body built by Alexander but to Leyland design. Two further Leyland double-deckers, numbered 26 and 27, arrived in 1947 and 1948. A significant event in 1949 was the introduction of an arrangement with Rawtenstall Corporation whereby both undertakings shared one General Manager. One effect of this was that numbering of new vehicles recommenced at number 1 although the Department remained faithful to Leyland for the remainder of its existence. Full details of the postwar deliveries are given in the fleet summary in Appendix 1. When Leyland Motors ceased manufacturing bus bodies in 1953, another local manufacturer, East Lancashire Coachbuilders of Blackburn supplied all the Department's new vehicle body requirements.

A notable exception to the normal policy of purchasing new occurred in 1962 and 1963 when two Leyland Royal Tiger single-deckers with Roe bodies were purchased secondhand from Ramsbottom UDC. From 1966 fleet numbering again reverted to start at 1.

It was announced in January 1963 that the Corporation had agreed to talks with Rawtenstall Corporation on the setting up of a Joint Transport Committee. Naturally, there were voices for and against the proposal and it was only the casting vote of the Mayor which saw the motion carried.

The amalgamation took place with effect from April 1968 and from the 15 Haslingden vehicles transferred to the new Joint Committee, only twelve received new fleet numbers to differentiate them from the former Rawtenstall vehicles. These were the former Haslingden buses numbered 1, 2, 5, 6, 9, 10 to 14, 17 and 18. Buses 4, 15 and 16 never operated for the new undertaking, and so did not receive new fleet numbers.

Rawtenstall Corporation Transport

On 16th December 1907 Rawtenstall Corporation began operation of a bus service along the Lumb Valley between Waterfoot and Water using a Ryknield double-deck bus. It carried 500 passengers during the first two days and the takings for the week were £20 – well above the figure of £12 needed to cover the cost. A similar bus started operation in February 1908, both vehicles carrying a blue and cream livery, but they proved to be unsatisfactory and the service ceased in September 1910. It was said that the unreliability of the buses meant that the Lumb buses had few friends. When the road was wet, they scattered mud and when it was dry they offended people by leaving trails of dust. The Bacup Times of 8th May 1909 observed:

'In order to realise what a dust storm may be like, readers should experience being on the road between Water and Waterfoot when the nuisance, owned by the Rawtenstall Corporation, and commonly known as the motor bus, has been passing. Not only would their eyes, ears, nose and throat have been filled, but also their clothes. In these days when we hear so much about micro laden dust and its effect on health, it is somewhat surprising to find an up-to-date (?) Corporation providing such a conveyance of disease to carry its burgesses, or at least some part of them, from place to place.'

A male passenger is reputed to have booked a stage at a time because he could never be sure of getting any further! One of the buses, registered FA 157, converted to a tower wagon, was retained until the end of tramway operation in 1932.

An early incident which occurred in connection with FA 159 arose from the desire of the members of the Bury and District Water Board to visit one of their reservoirs in July 1908. They obtained permission from the Chairman of Rawtenstall Corporation Tramways Committee to use the bus for the day but while it was going down Cog Lane

Rawtenstall Corporation's first bus was this 1907 Ryknield, registered FA 157, which was normally used on a service between Waterfoot and Water. It is said that its unreliability made a mockery of timetables, and it was referred to by some as 'that nuisance'. It seems to have a good load here, possibly at the inauguration of the service and before its unreliability became apparent and widely known. *(RMC)*

in Burnley the brakes failed and it ran away down the hill. At the junction with Coal Clough Lane, it hit a cart carrying rocks and crashed into a wall. In the collision several of the passengers were injured. One of the passengers brought an action for damages against Rawtenstall Town Council. The Lord Chief Justice, after considering the matter ruled that the Chairman did not have the authority to hire out the vehicle and there was therefore no contract with the Corporation and the case was dismissed. He did, however, comment, before reaching this verdict, that the bus was thoroughly unroadworthy and therefore a nuisance on the road.

On 1st January 1908, the Corporation acquired the portion of the Accrington Steam Tramway Company's line that was within the Borough boundary. On 1st October 1908 the Rawtenstall and Bacup Councils jointly purchased the Rossendale Steam Tramway Company and commenced electrification of the line. During the work on the conversion from steam to electric traction, a serious accident occurred on 24th December 1908. An engine had to be changed from the front to the rear of a car near Lockgate and when it was uncoupled the car ran backwards down a long incline. The brakes were unable to check it and after it had run some distance, two of the passengers jumped off. One of them was killed and the other seriously injured. The car was brought to a stop by crashing into another one which was standing empty. Several of the passengers who had remained on the runaway car were injured in the collision.

It was reported in March 1909 that work was well advanced for the conversion from steam to electric traction and that negotiations were taking place with Haslingden Council to facilitate through running from Bacup to Accrington via Rawtenstall and Haslingden. In June 1909 it was further reported that Haslingden was willing, but that there were problems with regard to Accrington and Rawtenstall reaching agreement. In October 1909 it was announced that agreement had been reached, but that Rawtenstall's agreement was for a twelve months trial period. Initial runs were made, with dead weights rather than with passengers, and the results were reported to be favourable and through running between Bacup and Accrington commenced on 1st April 1910.

Steam trams continued to operate until 22nd July 1909 when operation ceased, this being the last regular operation of a street steam tramway in Britain. Operation of the electric tramways was covered by the Rawtenstall Corporation Tramways Act 1907, the wording of which suggests that it was the intention to carry goods as well as passengers and the following clause from the Act covered this :

'The tramways may be used for the carriage of passengers, animals, goods, articles and things at the rates or charges not exceeding the rate per mile following:-

> For every horse, mule or other beast of draught or burden, fourpence.
> For every ox, cow, bull or head of cattle threepence.
> For every calf, pig or sheep or small animal one penny halfpenny.
> For all coal, coke, culm, charcoal, cannel, limestone, chalk, lime, salt, sand, fireclay cinders, dung, compost, and all sorts of manure per ton, twopence. Various other commodities are quoted at 2½d, 3d, and 4d per ton per mile whilst carriages of any description were one shilling.'

On 17th August 1908 the first setts were taken up at Crawshawbooth by the Mayor, Councillor Cryer and the Chairman of the Tramways Committee, Councillor Coupe, to mark the inauguration of the electric tramway system. The first section of electric tramway to open was that to Crawshawbooth and the newly constructed extension to Loveclough, this heading north towards Burnley. This section was inspected by the Board of Trade on Thursday 10th December 1908 and although intended for electric operation, as an interim measure, an hourly service of steam trams was operated. This was thought to be the last section of new steam tramway to be opened in Britain. However, Burnley was never reached for despite proposals to extend the Rawtenstall system to Burnley's Summit terminus, nothing came of it and the termini were connected initially by a horse bus service operated by a Mr Hargreaves until it was replaced by a motor bus service.

On Saturday 15th May 1909, Rawtenstall commenced electric tramway operation between Lockgate, Rawtenstall and Disley's Woollen Mill, Waterbarn and between Rawtenstall and Loveclough. Steam trams continued between Waterbarn and Bacup. The opening of the scheme which had cost £120,000 was made an occasion of public demonstration. In the morning Mr Coupe,

Chairman of the Tramways Committee, declared the power station open. The municipal party then travelled over the routes in three tramcars which were driven by Mrs Grimshaw, the Mayoress, Mrs Coupe and Mrs Cryer, ex-Mayoress. Crowds of people watched the passage of the cars. Subsequently, the Mayor gave a luncheon at which appropriate toasts were honoured.

The formal Board of Trade inspection of the Waterbarn to Bacup section took place on Tuesday 20th July 1909 and operation commenced on Friday 23rd July. It was reported that Bacup officials made their way to Thrutch in the last steam tram and returned by electric tram.

At a meeting of Rawtenstall Town Council on 19th September 1909 a petition was presented from 1,285 ratepayers in the Whitewell Valley asking the council to construct a tramway in their locality. The petition, which arose from the problems with the motor buses previously mentioned, was favourably received and the Town Clerk was instructed to take steps to obtain a provisional order to cover the laying and working of a tramway in the Whitewell Valley.

On 20th November 1909 the Corporation advertised for tenders covering advertising rights on the tramcars.

The extension to Water in the form of a branch from the Bacup line at Waterfoot was opened on 21st January 1911, thus completing the tramway system with a total length of 11.75 miles. The opening inspired John Lord to write two poems one of which begins and ends:

> 'Hurrah ! Thrice repeated we shout as we witness,
> The cars in the valley so useful and fine,
> We're charmed by their advent, their movement and fitness,
> And shout as they curve and career on the line.
> The people of Whitewell in chorus delighted,
> Rejoice in the signs of advancement displayed,
> All points in the valley have now been united,
> From Water Co-op to Trickett's arcade.'

In 1910 a driver earned 6¾d per hour for a week of 60 hours and the conductor was paid a penny less per hour.

The initial rolling stock comprised 16 double-deck cars numbered 1-16, all balcony top-covered supplied by the United Electric Company of Preston and these were followed in 1912 by two further enclosed double-deck cars numbered 17 and 18. The first 16 cars were of the regenerative control type but their maintenance proved costly in relation to the power generated and later cars were of the normal Siemens type, a decision no doubt influenced by the report on the accident at Baxenden Brow detailed in the next paragraph. Also supplied in 1912 were six single-deck cars numbered 19-24 which were fitted with magnetic and slipper brakes primarily for use on the steep route to Water. In 1922 a further eight double-deck fully enclosed cars, built by Brush and numbered 25-32, became the last cars to be purchased.

A notable accident occurred on Saturday 11th November 1911 which was to have repercussions on tramway operation throughout the country. Car No. 14 driven by Francis Cuff of Rawtenstall and with E Warwick of Rawtenstall as conductor, left Haslingden for Accrington at 10.35pm and all was well until they reached Baxenden Brow when the car ran away and collided with car No. 11 travelling in the opposite direction and driven by James Taylor of Rawtenstall with Charles Whittaker of Crawshawbooth as conductor. Both tramcars were extensively damaged and 16 people sustained injury, but fortunately none of the injuries were serious. A Board of Trade enquiry into the accident took place at the Municipal Offices, Rawtenstall, the following Wednesday 15th November where it was determined that the cause was failure of the regenerative braking system. Arising from this a ban was placed on the use of this system throughout the country.

Reference has previously been made to the carriage of livestock and goods. Just before midnight on 25th September 1916, a dull droning noise was heard in the skies above Bacup, and then moved down the valley towards Rawtenstall. It was a German Zeppelin which had misjudged its target of Manchester. An incendiary bomb fell into the grounds of Heightside House and was removed by a Special Constable who carried it some distance to the main road where he caught a tram to the police station. How would the present day Health and Safety Executive deal with this?

Ribble Motor Services had commenced operation in Preston in 1919 and soon indicated its desire to extend its area of operation. It had already reached Blackburn when, in September 1923, it applied for licences to operate a route from Burnley through Rawtenstall to Bolton, to Bury and to Rochdale as well as a route from Burnley to Todmorden via Bacup. Rawtenstall was not happy with this situation and declined to issue licences but decided to promote a Parliamentary Bill to operate its own motor buses. Bacup also declined to issue a licence to Ribble but approved the issue of a licence to Todmorden to operate a service from Todmorden to Burnley via Bacup.

The Corporation received powers from Parliament to operate buses along any route outside the Borough, subject to the consent of the Minister of Transport and of the authorities through whose area the routes were to pass. It was reported in January 1924 that the Corporation had sought authority for an expenditure of £20,000 for the provision of buses and a further £15,000 for the provision of accommodation. In due course application was made for consent to Burnley Corporation and a deputation was sent from Rawtenstall to meet a sub-committee appointed by Burnley Corporation. Burnley Corporation would not entertain the idea of Rawtenstall buses travelling down Manchester Road, Burnley on the grounds of competition with their trams and the dangerous nature of the road. Rawtenstall Corporation appealed to the Minister of Transport and an enquiry was held at Rawtenstall to consider the appeal and also an application from Ribble Motor Services to operate omnibuses along the same route. The Minister of Transport upheld the decision of Burnley Corporation against buses operating down Manchester Road on the grounds of danger in descending the steep hill.

The first Rawtenstall motor bus services, apart from the experimental and short lived service to Water in 1907, operated on 9th August 1924 from Rawtenstall to Newchurch and from Rawtenstall to Burnley via Loveclough but due to the refusal of Burnley Council to issue the necessary licence for Rawtenstall to operate within the Borough of Burnley the bus service had to terminate at Summit, where connection was made with the Burnley tram service. The initial motor bus fleet comprised six Leyland SG9 single-deckers painted in a maroon and cream livery with gold lining out and numbered 33-38, following directly on from the tram numbers. The tram depot on the north side of Bacup Road was extended in 1924 to accommodate buses.

Ramsbottom Urban District Council had operated a service from Edenfield to Rawtenstall Railway Station and this was acquired by Rawtenstall on 1st September 1924 together with two Thornycroft buses. Rawtenstall extended this service southwards to Bury and also linked it to the service to Burnley Summit. The through service commenced on 21st November 1924 and was operated jointly by Rawtenstall and Bury Corporations and Ramsbottom Urban District Council. This extension ceased on 31st March 1932, thereafter operating between Rawtenstall and Bury.

A further six Leyland single-deck buses were bought between 1925 and 1927 which enabled the introduction, in 1928, of an express bus service from Bacup to Accrington via Rawtenstall and Haslingden, jointly operated by the three Corporations. This service had, of course, its effect on the tram service and in 1929 the decision was taken to abandon the tram system. The trams on this route were replaced by the bus service on 1st May 1930 from which date the bus service was changed from express to stage carriage. Following this, the other tram routes ceased, that to Loveclough in 1931 and that to Water on 31st March 1932. However, the official closing ceremony did not take place until 7th April 1932. Further buses were required to replace the trams and a further six Leyland single-deckers were obtained along with the first double-deckers to be purchased, in 1931. These were four Leyland Titan TD1s, numbered 53-56, also carried highbridge Leyland bodywork, a combination that was to be repeated until the outbreak of the Second World War.

In 1930 there had been further representation to Burnley Corporation on the grounds that, due to improvements in bus design, the objections previously raised on the grounds of safety were no longer valid. Burnley Corporation accepted this and granted permission for Rawtenstall to operate their buses down Manchester Road subject to a financial agreement between Rawtenstall and Burnley regarding receipts and expenses of operation. The service through to Burnley operated during August 1930 but was withdrawn due to objections from Ribble Motor Services Ltd claiming an equal right to participate in services operated into Burnley on this route.

In the meantime an application by Burnley to operate outside their Borough was opposed by Ribble Motor Services Ltd and the Minister of Transport suspended the Inquiry until an arrangement could be made between Ribble and

Rawtenstall Corporation. A meeting between Ribble and Rawtenstall duly took place and resulted in a co-ordinated scheme being agreed upon whereby their two routes into Burnley were pooled on an agreed basis. Ribble and Rawtenstall then approached Burnley Corporation and offered to them similar terms to those obtaining when the Corporation was operating via Manchester Road to Burnley Cattle Market. These terms were declined by Burnley and no agreement was reached.

This was the situation when the Road Traffic Act 1930 came into operation after which application for road service licences to operate omnibus services had to be made to the Traffic Commissioners.

Agreement as to the co-ordination of omnibus services was made with Ribble Motor Services Ltd on 23rd March 1931, the preamble to which reads as follows:

'Whereas the respective parties hereto for some time past have each operated separate passenger transport services in various districts in competition with each other, and in order to eliminate such competition they have mutually agreed to provide for a system of transport co-ordination on the terms and in the manner hereinafter appearing.'

In the late 1920s Leyland Motors were busy promoting their new Titan bus using the slogan 'when you bury a tram, mark the spot with a Titan!' It was not often they had the chance to bury a *steam* tram and an electric one, and their photographer was duly despatched to record the event. Alderman Ashworth, in bowler hat, has been joined by Manager Frank Lythgoe. The last electric service tram ran on 31st March 1932. *(RMC)*

At the date of this agreement, efforts were still being made to break down Burnley's opposition to the extension of the Rawtenstall - Loveclough - Summit service into Burnley and provision for the extension which took place shortly afterwards was contained in this agreement.

A further bus route from Waterfoot to Cowpe had been introduced but was suspended because of a disagreement with Bacup Council. In June 1930 Bacup Council agreed to Rawtenstall operating services within its boundary and a route from Waterfoot to Britannia via Stacksteads and New Line commenced.

From this time the Rawtenstall route network settled down and remained unchanged for some time, but as patronage increased the earlier single-deck vehicles were gradually replaced with double-deckers. From 1932, following the demise of the trams, fleet numbering for double-deck vehicles

DTJ 57, No. 36, was one of two Leyland-bodied Leyland TD5c models (*ie* chassis fitted with torque-convertor transmission) delivered in 1939, these being the last pre-war double-deckers to enter the fleet. It is shown in Rawtenstall in June 1951. The pair each gave 20 years service before being withdrawn in 1959. *(RM)*

reverted to number 1 and by the end of the decade a further 36 such vehicles, numbered 1 to 36, had been purchased new. Single-deck fleet numbers kept to the old number series and filled numbers left vacant by withdrawals. By 1939, five single-decks numbered 45, 46 and 50-52 had been added to the fleet. All purchases, whether single-deck or double-deck were, of course, Leyland products.

Originally, buses were accommodated in the tram depot, but a new depot was built on the opposite side of Bacup Road and was officially opened on Monday 1st May 1933 by Councillor R Ashworth, Chairman of the Transport and Electricity Committee. Inside the depot, there was a platform decorated in the livery colours of the Corporation and with the word 'Progress' at the back and front of the platform.

Following this the north side tram depot closed, with just the offices retained.

The entrance to the new depot proclaimed 'Rawtenstall Corporation Motors' and this was used as a trading name for the bus operation from this time until the creation of the Joint Transport Committee in 1968. An extension was later added, and this was commissioned in 1938 with commemorative stonework suitably affixed. This can still be seen today in a prominent position opposite the bus station.

With the outbreak of the Second World War there came restrictions on the purchase of new buses and Rawtenstall was only allowed to purchase one new bus. Leyland Motors was not allowed to manufacture buses at this time and the vehicle allocated by the Ministry of War Transport was a Guy Arab with highbridge 'utility' body by Massey Brothers of Wigan. The Guy Arab was noted for its rugged simplicity and this vehicle remained in the fleet, despite being non-standard, for 21 years, receiving a new body by East Lancashire Coachbuilders of Blackburn in 1951.

In the nineteen forties, Mr S G McCrone was an electrician with Rawtenstall Corporation Transport and he developed an idea for a continuous contact strip for the operation of the bells used to give starting and stopping signals to the driver. The system was a great success and manufacture commenced on a part time basis in 1948 followed by a move to Crosthwaite, near Kendal in 1956 to place the company on a full time basis. The company was sold in 1989 becoming Cronopress Co. Ltd and later sold to a Mr C M Butler, who renamed it Cronopress Ltd.

Deliveries of Leyland vehicles continued after the war and 1947 saw the arrival of three Leyland PD1 double-decks, numbered 38-40, and the first PD2s, a batch of seven. The following year's Leyland PD2 vehicle intake was notable for two reasons, as not only was number 11 built on the first production PD2 double-deck chassis but, for the first time, these buses were fitted with bodies supplied by East Lancashire Coachbuilders. Single-deck purchases comprised four Leyland Tigers, two delivered in 1949 (numbered 53-4) and two in 1950 (numbered 55-6). All four had East Lancs bodies.

Following a Union meeting which had been held after the end of services on Saturday 28th August 1948, Mr Herbert Beaumont was driving colleagues home in a Corporation bus in the early hours of Sunday morning when the headlights of the bus picked up what looked like a bundle in the road. Upon investigation, it was found to be the body of a woman, later identified as Nancy Ellen Chadwick, who appeared to have been murdered. Subsequently, Margaret Allen, better known locally as Maggie Smith who, incidentally, had worked for Rawtenstall Corporation Transport as a clippie from July 1942 to June 1946, was found guilty of murder and sentenced to death. She was hanged at Strangeways Prison, Manchester on 12th January 1949, the first female execution in Britain for 12 years.

A significant event took place in 1949 when, as mentioned earlier, the General Manager of Rawtenstall, LT Merrall, also assumed the role of General Manager of Haslingden Corporation Transport. In 1951 he was, in addition, appointed General Manager of Ramsbottom Urban District Council Transport Department. Various schemes were considered over the following years to amalgamate the three undertakings and this was partly achieved with effect from 1st April 1968 when Haslingden and Rawtenstall Corporation Transport Departments combined to form the Rossendale Joint Transport Committee. Ramsbottom declined to become involved in this amalgamation and remained independent until November 1969 when it became part of the South East Lancashire and North East Cheshire Passenger Transport Executive (SELNEC).

In common with Haslingden, it was now time to restart numbering from number 1 and in the subsequent period up to 1953, a total of 26 additional PD2s were acquired, initially bodied by Leyland but then by East Lancs when the production of Leyland bodies ceased in 1953.

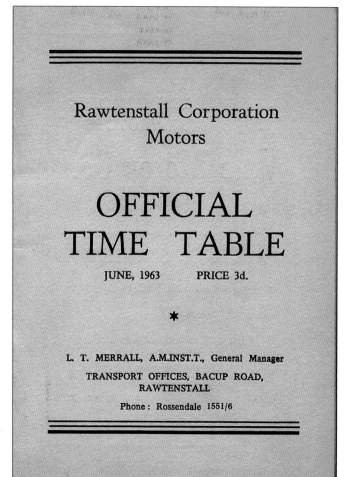

Rawtenstall Corporation Motors

OFFICIAL TIME TABLE

JUNE, 1963   PRICE 3d.

*

L. T. MERRALL, A.M.INST.T., General Manager

TRANSPORT OFFICES, BACUP ROAD, RAWTENSTALL

Phone : Rossendale 1551/6

Cover of a 1963 time table showing the by then quaintly named undertaking – the name having been adopted 30 years earlier following the demise of the tramcars. *(BD)*

The first of these were numbered 1-20 but the decision to restart numbering was perhaps a little premature and new deliveries in 1953 were unable to take their allotted numbers of 21-3 because they were still being used by the earlier TD4s. They were consequently numbered 24-6. Things got worse and the 1955 arrivals had to be numbered 60-5. Only in January 1964 were these problems resolved when buses 24-6 became 21-3 and the 60-5 batch were renumbered 24-9.

New single-deck deliveries followed the previous practice of numbering upwards from the original series and a Leyland Tiger Cub demonstrator, numbered 57, arrived in 1955, fitted with a Weymann body instead of the normal East Lancs bodies which were fitted to the next two Tiger Cubs. These carried fleet numbers 58/9 upon their delivery in 1958 and 1960 respectively.

The Department celebrated its Golden Jubilee with the publication of a booklet, 'The Golden Jubilee of the Rawtenstall Corporation Transport Department 1908-1958'. Strictly speaking the Jubilee was the previous year, operations having commenced in December 1907.

In common with the policy at Haslingden, 1963 saw the arrival from the Ramsbottom fleet of a secondhand Leyland Royal Tiger with Roe body. A spare fleet number (52) was used for this vehicle.

The 1964 deliveries, comprising two of the new Leopard chassis, used fleet numbers 50 and 51.

The first Leyland PD3s with forward entrance bodywork by East Lancs arrived in 1964. Numbered 30-3, these were followed by similar examples 34-7 in 1965 and 38-41 delivered in 1966.

April 1968 saw the transfer of all vehicles to a new Joint Committee covering the operations of Haslingden and Rawtenstall. Whilst Haslingden vehicles were renumbered upon transfer, Rawtenstall vehicles retained their existing fleet numbers and their contribution to the enlarged fleet comprised double-decks numbered 1-10 and 16-42 together with single-decks 50-2 and 55-9.

The 1964 delivery of double-deckers, the first since 1955, marked a return to the exposed radiator, the increase in length to 30ft, and the adoption of a front entrance. The order comprised four Leyland PD3/4 with East Lancashire Coachbuilders bodies numbered 30 - 3. This nearside view of No.31, taken near Rossendale Hospital in March 1966, clearly shows the sliding door.
(RM)

Rossendale Joint Transport Committee / Rossendale Borough Transport

The establishment of the Rossendale Joint Transport Committee in 1968 brought together 15 vehicles from the Haslingden fleet, in a blue and cream livery, and 45 vehicles from the Rawtenstall fleet in their crimson lake and cream livery. Of the acquisitions, two Rawtenstall buses and three Haslingden buses were not used in service and so the initial fleet strength stood at 55 vehicles. It was agreed to adopt the Rawtenstall livery for the enlarged fleet and the Haslingden depot in John Street was closed with all operations moved to Rawtenstall's 1933 bus depot. It has been said that, from the staff point of view, the merger went very well from the outset. There were no 'us and them' attitudes and everyone was keen to work together for the new undertaking.

Seen leaving Rawtenstall for Newchurch in September 1968, and carrying the 'Joint Transport Committee' fleetname, is the former Rawtenstall Leyland Titan PD2 RTE 537, by now renumbered 23. *(RM)*

A fire broke out at the Bacup Road Depot in April 1972 as fuel was being unloaded from a tanker into storage tanks. The alarm was raised by Mr Ralph Petterson, the emergency shift man and drivers Robert Trickett, Robert Edwards and John Rowen moved a number of vehicles out of the depot. Fortunately, no one was injured and the only damage to the vehicles remaining in the depot was from the effects of smoke. Above the fuelling area, part of the depot roof was damaged and, to this day, the replacement sections can still be distinguished from the original part of the garage.

With local government reorganisation in 1974 and the establishment of the Borough of Rossendale, the Joint Transport Committee became Rossendale Borough Transport.

From the amalgamation of the two undertakings, vehicle purchasing policy continued as before with Leyland chassis and East Lancashire Coachbuilders bodies being purchased. With the move towards one-person operation, single-deckers started to be more significant and initially Leyland Leopard chassis were purchased with East Lancashire Coachbuilders bodies. One of the five such vehicles purchased in 1973 was fitted with coach seating in 1982, classified as 'dual-purpose' and used to advertise 'Rossendale Coach Hire'. The vehicle concerned, No. 5, had the distinction

of being the first Rossendale vehicle to venture overseas, when it undertook a private hire to Brittany in April 1984.

The Leyland Leopard had an excellent reputation for reliability but it was a high floor chassis, more suited to coaches than buses where passengers were frequently getting on and off. By now, rear-engined single-deckers which afforded lower and easier access were established, and, of those available, the Bristol RE was generally regarded as the best. It was not surprising, therefore, when, in 1974, Rossendale purchased its first Bristol chassis in the form of five RE models fitted with bodies by East Lancashire Coachbuilders. Four similar vehicles followed in 1975, but two of these were painted in a new livery to promote private hire activities and fitted with 'semi-luxury' dual-purpose seating. The association with Leyland was, however, continued by the fact that these Bristol chassis were powered by Leyland engines. Paradoxically, at the same time, the neighbouring authorities of Accrington and Burnley were buying Leopards instead of their earlier Bristol RE purchases.

The 1977 order for the first rear-engined Rossendale double-deckers called for Gardner engined Bristol VRTs, but materialised in the form of three Leyland Atlanteans with bodies by East Lancashire Coachbuilders. These initial Atlanteans were numbered 15-7 and were followed by a further eleven examples, numbered 18-28, in the years up to 1982. In addition to introducing driver-only operation of double-deckers, the replacement of the Leyland PD3 fleet also commenced.

Rossendale had never used service numbers but these were introduced in 1977 with the delivery of the Atlanteans. The Accrington to Bacup service was numbered 4 as this was the number used by Hyndburn and previously by Accrington. Other local services received low route numbers.

In 1980 a major change took place in the passenger transport industry with the deregulation of long-distance coach services, and a number of operators saw this as an opportunity to provide such services in competition with National Express. Burnley and Pendle Transport established a service from Colne to London, marketed as the City Flyer and operated jointly with Leicester and Maidstone Corporations. From Friday 13th August 1982, Rossendale provided a feeder service from Ramsbottom via Haslingden, Rawtenstall and Bacup to connect with this service at Todmorden. Passengers expecting a high specification coach were to be disappointed, however, as Rossendale used its coach-seated Bristol RE number 12 on the very first journey and

Number 60, ETC 660J, a Leyland Leopard with East Lancashire Coachbuilders body, was purchased by the Joint Committee in 1971 and is shown in Haslingden in May 1971. Note the short length, giving a 'stubby' appearance by today's standards. *(RM)*

thereafter the service used the coach-seated Leopard or REs for the journey to Todmorden.

A notable occurrence in March 1982 was the appearance of a British Leyland-DAB articulated bus demonstrator which was used for a week's trials on various trunk routes operated by Rossendale Transport. The vehicle concerned, sporting 'Cityliner' livery, had been hired from South Yorkshire PTE, in whose fleet it was numbered 2008.

The move towards one-person operation continued and was eventually completed in 1982. It did, however, present a problem on the service from Rawtenstall to Cowpe due to the limited space available at Cowpe for the turning of the vehicle. In the past this had involved the assistance of the conductor. The problem was overcome by the purchase of 2 short Bristol LHS single-deckers with 28-seat bodies by East Lancashire Coachbuilders. These were the only examples of this chassis and body combination and some of the last LH models to enter service. So it was that on Saturday 12th June 1982, the words, "Fares please" were uttered for the last time when conductor Edmund Scholes and driver Armando 'Joe' Teoli took Leopard number 53 on the 10.50pm turn from Rawtenstall to Hall Carr. Edmund, together with the last remaining conductress, Rita Booth, both continued to work for the company as customer relations staff, dealing with market research.

In the early 'eighties Lancashire County Council was keen to co-ordinate bus services in the County and various agency agreements were established with the National Bus Company local operator, Ribble Motor Services, and the various municipal undertakings in Lancashire. As part of this move, a new route pattern was established in Rossendale and came into effect on Sunday 13th June 1982. This involved services between Bury and Bolton in the south and Burnley in the north, operating through Rossendale. Also involved was Greater Manchester Transport which provided services to the south of Rossendale as successor to the former Bury and Ramsbottom municipal undertakings.

Arising from this reorganisation, route 291, operated jointly by Rossendale and Ribble between Rawtenstall and Burnley via Crawshawbooth, was withdrawn. There was also a proposal to withdraw Ribble route 236 between Bolton and Burnley via Ramsbottom, Edenfield, Rawtenstall and Water but following objections from residents of the Lumb Valley, it was agreed to retain a shortened route 236 between Rawtenstall and Burnley via Water. Through facilities between Bolton and Burnley were provided by new route 273 operating via Ramsbottom, Edenfield, Rawtenstall and Crawshawbooth. This service operated hourly and was supplemented between Rawtenstall and Burnley by the diversion of service 473 to operate via Bury, Edenfield, Rawtenstall, Crawshawbooth and Burnley rather than by its previous route, north east of Rawtenstall, to the terminus at Water. Together, services 273 and 473 provided a 30 minute headway between Rawtenstall and Burnley. South of Rawtenstall service 473 was augmented by short journeys to provide a 30 minute headway. Rossendale, Ribble and Greater Manchester Transport (successors to Bury Corporation Transport Department) operated jointly on all sections of these routes and it is interesting to note that these revisions re-introduced a through service between Bury and Burnley via Rawtenstall, a facility which Ribble Motor Services and Rawtenstall Corporation had battled over in 1924. It was also the first time that Rossendale had operated to Bolton and the honour of working the first journey fell to Atlantean 28. Details of the routes and the operators involved together with local Rossendale routes are given in Appendix 2.

With the introduction of the new route pattern, Lancashire County Council was able to negotiate the elimination of the former protected area within Burnley. This removed the restriction that had been in force since the 1930 Act. Another important change at this time was that limited stop service 743, operated by Ribble between Manchester and Burnley via Bury and Rawtenstall, was enhanced by the introduction of additional local stopping places, which enabled long-distance passengers to reduce journey times.

As part of the agency agreement, Rossendale received a subsidy from Lancashire County Council and this was used to invest in the business. New garage pits were provided together with a new bus wash, new electronic ticket machines and refurbishment of Rawtenstall bus station.

The end of two-person operation also meant the end for the remaining Leyland Titan PD3 double-deckers and on Saturday 20th November 1982, fleet numbers 39 and 46 participated in a 'Leyland PD3 Farewell Tour', bringing to an end an era of 51 years during which front-engined Leyland double-deckers had given service to the people of Rossendale. The tour also celebrated 75 years of municipal transport and almost 150 passengers boarded the two buses, which were operated by George and Rita Booth on ex-Haslingden bus 46 with Roy Berry and Frank Scholes on ex-Rawtenstall 39. Both buses saw sporadic service after this date on some swimming baths contracts and the local Asda superstore free bus service, but were finally retired at the end of 1982. They were also the last of the pre-Joint Transport Committee fleet to operate in service and their passing also marked the point where the fleet was at its most standardised, in that every bus in service at this time had a registration number that corresponded with the fleet number and all had ELCB bodies.

The introduction of one-person operation also had a human effect for conductors were no longer required. Roy Berry had spent 35 years as a conductor on the buses and along with other conductors was offered driver training. Of this opportunity Roy is reported as saying, "I had a go at driving and put the fear of God up myself and the passengers; it wasn't for me". Roy's good service to the undertaking was recognised and he was provided with a job in the depot. His interest, however, extended beyond conducting and he became much in demand for presenting talks on his experiences 'on the buses'.

A further Bristol LHS, albeit longer than the previous two and seating 35, was purchased secondhand from London Country in 1983. This bus, which had been new in 1977, was fitted with a body by Eastern Coach Works of Lowestoft.

Previous reference has been made to the desire of Lancashire County Council to promote bus services in the county. This took a further step forward from 3rd October 1983 with the introduction of the Red Rose Rambler Ticket. This ticket, which cost £12.50 and was valid for one week, could be used on trains and bus services of all operators in the County of Lancashire. It was valid after 9.15am on Mondays to Fridays and all day on Saturdays, Sundays and Bank Holidays. One child travelled free when accompanied by an

Leyland Atlantean No. 28, dating from 1982, shows the new livery with the 'green hills' symbol as it operates service 291 in Burnley in April 1982 – shortly after entering service. *(RM)*

adult and for other children there was a Child Ticket priced at £6.25. A number of buses from various operators received overall advertisements for the ticket and Rossendale Leyland Atlantean No. 24 was so treated.

Further integration of services occurred in October 1983 when a number of separate local services were combined into a new hourly service operating between Balladen, Hall Carr, Rawtenstall, Staghills, Newchurch, Stacksteads and Bacup. From the same date Rossendale ventured outside the Borough boundary to provide a two hourly service between Sharneyford, Bacup, Weir and Burnley, together with another service operating from Burnley to Water, Rawtenstall and Oakley.

Because of the termination of the government's 'New Bus Grant' it was decided to suspend purchase of new double-deck buses and instead three nine-year-old Leyland Atlantean double-deckers with Alexander panoramic windowed bodies were purchased from Strathclyde Passenger Transport Executive during 1984.

Two short Bristol LHS 28-seat midibuses with East Lancashire bodies were purchased in 1982, primarily for the service to Cowpe, which involved the use of narrow roads and with restricted turning space. They were numbered 50/51, and the latter was photographed at Waterfoot in July 1982. *(RM)*

New technology arrived at the company on 20th May 1984 when Almex Timtronic electronic ticket machines were installed on all Rossendale buses at a total cost of £110,000.

A major departure from previous practice took place in 1985 when Rossendale's first coaches, three Leyland Leopards numbered 80 (later renumbered to 86), 81 and 82, with coach bodies by Plaxton, were purchased from Hills of Tredegar, South Wales, these having been new in 1981/2. Two further Plaxtons were acquired from Hills of Tredegar during 1986 but these were more modern Leyland Tigers, fitted with air suspension.

On Monday 14th January 1985, the Transport Department offices moved from the former tram depot offices on the north of Bacup Road to new offices constructed internally within the bus depot on the south of Bacup Road. This enabled the Rossendale Borough Council Treasurer's Department to transfer from Haslingden and the former tram offices were subsumed into an enlarged town hall complex.

The publication of the 1985 Transport Act was to have a major effect on passenger transport operators throughout the country. On the one hand it proposed the privatisation of the National Bus Company and on the other hand the deregulation of local bus services, thus removing the protection from direct competition, which local bus service operators had enjoyed under the 1930 Transport Act. In practice, this meant that operators, both

established and new, could register any local bus service which they believed could be operated commercially (at a profit). Operators were no longer allowed to cross-subsidise services and only where the transport authority (County Council or PTE) considered that the level of service did not meet a particular social need, was it allowed discretion to invite tenders for the provision of the service or journeys concerned. From the same time, the Restrictive Trade Practices Act 1976 was now to apply to bus services and so meant that the operation of a joint service by two or more operators or any joint fares marketing schemes needed to be registered with the Office of Fair Trading.

Local authorities were required to divest themselves of their transport undertakings, either to form separate arms-length limited liability companies or to sell to private companies. Faced with the possibility of new operators registering what they saw as profitable services, many local authorities decided to sell their transport departments but Rossendale Borough Council decided to retain control of its transport undertaking and an arms-length company, Rossendale Transport Limited, was formally

incorporated with effect from 27th March 1986 and commenced trading on 26th October 1986.

Lancashire County Council was very much against the 1985 Transport Act and published, in January 1985, a series of leaflets covering the various areas of the county under the general heading 'Your bus service is under attack.' On the back of the leaflet there was a letter from Councillor Mrs Louise Ellman, Chair of Lancashire County Council in which she suggested that the people of Lancashire may like to contact their Members of Parliament and voice their concerns over the proposed changes. Despite this, the Bill was passed and came into force on 26th October 1986.

Prior to this, however, by 28th February 1986, all operators were required to register, with the Traffic Commissioner, details of all services that they intended to operate commercially from

Chief Engineer Tom Swift stands proudly by new East Lancashire-bodied Leyland Atlantean No. 25 following its delivery in 1980. *(RT)*

'Deregulation Day'. Details of all these services were listed in a special issue of Notices & Proceedings dated 27th March 1986.

This presented a particular problem to the officers and councillors of Rossendale Borough Council as there was still a major part of the Borough not served by Rossendale buses. Since 1974, Whitworth had been part of the Borough of Rossendale but buses in this part of the Borough were provided by Greater Manchester Transport, as the successors to Rochdale Corporation Transport Department, who had operated buses between Rochdale and Bacup via Whitworth since March 1928.

In common with most existing north-west operators, Rossendale decided to operate as much as possible of the existing route pattern on a commercial basis. Generally, daytime services and Thursday, Friday and Saturday evening services were deemed to be commercial. Joint operations were to continue with Hyndburn Transport (formerly Accrington Corporation) on service 4 between Bacup and Accrington but Greater Manchester Transport declined to participate in the 273 and 473 operations as they did not wish to continue their operations to Burnley. Consequently, 273 was to be jointly operated by Rossendale and Ribble on an hourly headway between Burnley and Bolton. South of Rawtenstall, Rossendale and Greater Manchester Transport agreed to operate a joint 15 minute headway service 472 between Rawtenstall and Bury via Ramsbottom and Walmersley, together with a similar joint 15 minute headway service on service 474 between Bury and Stubbins via Brandlesholme.

Calculations showed that no school buses could be operated commercially and Rossendale Transport calculated that losses of £300,000 a year would be made unless school hours could be staggered so that one bus could serve at least two schools. Faced with this scenario, school times were altered so that those in the west of the Borough generally had earlier hours than those in the east.

All was well until just before the deadline date for final registrations when Rossendale discovered that Greater Manchester Transport was to extend its Rochdale to Bacup service through to Rawtenstall. Whilst Rossendale took the brave step to register a 30 minute headway service between Bacup and Rochdale in order to serve the whole of the Borough, some sense prevailed and Rossendale buses operated 'on the other half hour' to provide a combined 15 minute headway between both companies. Needless to say these decisions were to have significant effects over the next few years and would greatly influence the future direction of the Rossendale undertaking.

A full list of the services registered for Deregulation Day is shown as Appendix 3.

Even with the additional service between Bacup and Rochdale, there was a need to reduce the size of the fleet and consequently the number of staff. Negotiations to effect these changes continued through 1986 but in parallel, the authorities at Lancashire County Council and GMPTE had identified a number of areas where they issued tenders for services or journeys to complement the commercial timetables registered by bus companies. Because of the ill-feeling caused by Rossendale's 'incursion' into Rochdale, the outcome of this tendering process was that GM Buses, as the successor to Greater Manchester Transport, was awarded (said to be at suicidal prices) nearly all the subsidised evening and Sunday services in Rossendale, together with trunk services between Rawtenstall and Blackburn, Burnley (via Water) and Rochdale, which had all formerly been operated by Ribble.

In contrast, Rossendale was awarded services in the Rochdale area which had previously been operated by Greater Manchester Transport. These were not just evenings and Sundays but included daytime services to Castleton and Sudden (hourly 432), Lane Head (hourly 439), Syke (30 minute 440), Shawclough (hourly 446), Peppermint Bridge and Littleborough (combined hourly 451, 452 via Milnrow).

Closer to home, Rossendale was awarded a Lancashire County Council contract to extend from Sharneyford over the hills and into Yorkshire to replace the Bacup to Todmorden service previously operated by buses of West Yorkshire Passenger Transport Executive.

The effect was that, rather than needing to make drivers redundant, there was now an urgent need to recruit and train existing staff for all the new services in the Rochdale area. Ironically, many drivers made redundant by Greater Manchester Transport were recruited by Rossendale. In order to cope with this increased training requirement, the preserved Leyland bodied Leyland PD2 double-decker No. 18 which had been re-acquired from Gerald Walker of Tower Coaches, Wigton, Cumbria a few years earlier saw more intensive use along with former Haslingden PD2 No. 44. In addition, two Leyland PD3 double-deckers were hired to provide additional capacity.

It was also clear that the size of the fleet would have to be increased to cope with the additional services that had been secured, in stark contrast to the early predictions of some of the consequences of deregulation, where a requirement of around 30 vehicles had been contemplated – a reduction of some one-third of the fleet strength.

Since 1985, the oldest Leyland Leopards had been progressively withdrawn and stored as they came up for their annual MOT tests. With the exception of the two most heavily cannibalised vehicles, these buses were brought back into service to provide some of the extra buses that would be required for 'Deregulation Day'. In addition to this, neighbouring Hyndburn Transport,

which had a surplus of vehicles at deregulation, were able to supply three of their oldest East Lancs bodied PDR1 Atlanteans. These vehicles arrived on the 21st October 1986 but did not operate until the new limited company began trading. Other arrivals from Hyndburn, but this time on short-term loan, were a Ford Transit minibus and a Bristol RE. The Transit remained on loan until the arrival of Rossendale's own order for three Freight Rover Sherpas.

Number 18, a 1953 Leyland PD2, was sold for preservation and then bought back. It was later used for driver training. It is shown here in Accrington on 15 June 1974 shortly after the formation of the Borough of Rossendale. *(RM)*

Rossendale Transport Limited

1986-90: The Battle for Survival

26th October 1986, generally referred to as 'Deregulation Day', was the first day of operation for the new arms-length company set up as Rossendale Transport Limited. The honour of being the first bus to leave the depot under the new regime fell to Leyland Leopard No. 4.

Greater Manchester Transport was re-branded as GM Buses and in order to promote the change, did so in a blaze of publicity which in Greater Manchester declared that, 'We'll pick you up tomorrow as usual'. In the Rossendale area, the material was entitled "The new look for the future" and declared that the people of Greater Manchester had received good service and good value from Greater Manchester Transport since 1974 – 'Now it's your turn'. Both claims were to be put to the test and by February 1987 there had been numerous complaints of services registered by GM Buses, failing to operate in Rossendale and in other areas controlled by Lancashire County Council.

There was regular hiring-in of additional vehicles from Hyndburn, some on a daily basis, but other vehicles were used for longer periods. The three Freight Rover Sherpa van-derived minibuses were used to supplement the Bristol LHs on local routes 7, 8, 9, 10 and 15 and were also used on some of the new contracted services.

The company was proud to discover that one of its drivers, Abdul Bhatti, had been awarded the British Empire Medal in the 1987 New Year's Honours List. At the time he had worked on the buses for 24 years, had been a former T&GWU chairman and was heavily involved in the Pakistani Welfare Association.

April 1987 saw the introduction of the final vehicle ordered by the former Rossendale Borough Transport. This was a 78 seat double-deck coach bodied by East Lancs and based on a Leyland Olympian chassis with a TL11 engine. Meant to perform both bus duties and private hire, it was painted in the Rossendale Coach Hire livery but proved to be a very troublesome vehicle, prone to engine overheating. This led to its premature demise in 1995, by which time it had been re-registered.

Between 'Deregulation Day' and 26th January 1987, operators were not allowed to make any changes to their registered services, but from that date, GM Buses doubled the frequency of service

Fleet number 1, a Leyland Leopard with ELCB bodywork supplied to the Joint Committee in 1973, was still giving good service 15 years later when photographed at Hall Carr in April 1988 in typical Rossendale scenery. *(RM)*

472 and extended it to Rawtenstall via Stubbins. So, from 15th March 1987 Rossendale Transport withdrew from jointly operated services 472 and 474 to concentrate on a new independently operated service 483 between Rawtenstall and Bury via Shuttleworth instead of Ramsbottom. Expansion in Rochdale continued with the introduction of an hourly service 435 between Rochdale and Buckstones (at GMPTE request and on the opposite 30 minutes to GM Buses' commercial hourly service). Services 451 and 452 were both increased to operate every hour and service 432 was extended from its Sudden terminus to provide circular services 431 and 432 to compete with GM Buses between Castleton and Rochdale.

In early 1987 GM Buses stepped up competition by running many duplicate journeys between Rochdale and Rawtenstall but in late 1987 a strange situation occurred when GM Buses applied to the Traffic Commissioner to withdraw completely from the Bacup to Rawtenstall section of route but then rescinded their decision. The Traffic Commissioner would not allow the service to recommence as a registered service until the expiry of the requisite 42 days' notice and this resulted in GM Buses continuing to operate the service unchanged but allowing passengers to travel free between Bacup and Rawtenstall for a period of two weeks. With effect from 30th November 1987, Rossendale gave up the use of service numbers 465 and 466 between Bacup and Rochdale to concentrate operations on a 30 minute

service 464 between Accrington, Bacup and Rochdale. Hyndburn Transport continued to operate journeys confined to the Accrington to Bacup section, which was subsequently increased from a joint 15 minute headway to 10 minutes from 29th February 1988.

To operate the competitive services, a number of used single- and double-deck buses were progressively acquired from December 1986 and, rather ironically, were former Greater Manchester PTE vehicles that had been rendered surplus as a result of Deregulation. The majority of the purchases were Daimler and Leyland Fleetlines with Northern Counties bodies to the GMT standard specification, full details of which are given in the fleet summary. They were also joined in the spring of 1987 by a pair of Duple-bodied Leopard coaches, one of which was no stranger to the district, having served with Ribble on the Manchester limited-stop services. In order to meet the demands of operators who were not happy with the lower standards of van-derived minibuses such as the Sherpas, Metro Cammell Weymann (MCW) produced a purpose designed minibus named the 'Metrorider'. After trying a demonstration vehicle to assess its suitability, Rossendale became an early supporter of this vehicle with an initial order for four vehicles, numbered from 56-59, which arrived in February 1988.

An omen for the future was the introduction from 29th February 1988 of commercial service P3 operating every 40 minutes between Accrington

and Haslingden, by a single vehicle of a new company called Pilkingtons. This was Rossendale Transport's first experience of competition from a small private operator which had not operated bus services prior to 1986, but whose older buses and smaller administrative costs meant that they could operate commercially at lower fares than the established operator. In retaliation, 'Farebuster' services were introduced but subsequently withdrawn when Pilkingtons withdrew on 24th October 1988.

From the same weekend, the GM Buses trunk services between Rawtenstall and Blackburn, Burnley (via Water) and Rochdale were taken over by Burnley and Pendle. Other GM Buses contracted local services in Rossendale were lost to Rossendale Transport from 5th April 1988.

Facing page: Number 55 was one of three Freight Rover minibuses purchased in 1987 from West Midlands PTE. It is shown in the centre of Rawtenstall heading for Irwell Vale in February 1987. *(RM)*

The Metro-Cammell-Weymann 'Metrorider' was a purpose designed and built minibus and Rossendale purchased eight of these in 1987/8. Number 57 was photographed in March 1988 at Irwell Vale negotiating an awkward turn and demonstrating why such small vehicles were needed for some services. *(RM)*

Competition increased from 5th April 1988, when GM Buses service 467 between Rochdale and Shawforth was withdrawn to concentrate on an increased 15 minute service between Rochdale and Bacup. Extensive publicity was produced and specially liveried vehicles proclaimed the route as 'The Whitworth Valley Way – Over 100 times a day.' In retaliation, Rossendale decided to expand into the GM Buses area and so, from 24th October 1988, they introduced a 30 minute Monday to Saturday daytime service, numbered 19, from Rochdale to Middleton via Castleton. Needless to say GM Buses introduced a similar service from 14th November. The period of retaliatory strikes had arrived.

From 1st August 1988, Rossendale used the Metroriders to commence operation of two new Monday to Saturday contracted services on behalf of GMPTE, service 441 operating every hour to Foxholes and service 442 to Castleton via Marland.

A notable addition at this time was an ex-Ribble Leyland Tiger, fleet number 80, which was fitted with a 49 seat Plaxton 3500 'Paramount' body to executive specification. This was the first coach fitted with a toilet and enabled Rossendale Coach Hire to operate journeys to Continental destinations such as Paris and Amsterdam. Other secondhand Leyland bus acquisitions were four Leopards from

Kelvin Scottish and five Tigers from Trimdon Motor Services and Hutchison of Overtown, and these joined the fleet from late 1987 onwards.

Sufficient confidence in the Company's operations justified the placing of an order for the first 'full-size' new buses later in 1988 and four new Leyland Tiger single-deckers with East Lancashire Coachbuilders bodies (fleet numbers 92-95) were delivered in January 1989. One of these was loaned back to East Lancashire Coachbuilders when the operator Midland Red North was considering rebodying a number of chassis with service bus bodies for use on a service which involved passing under two low and narrow railway bridges near the village of Little Haywood in Staffordshire. Rossendale No. 93 was driven very carefully under the bridges and emerged without mishap. Arising from this East Lancashire Coachbuilders received an order from Midland Red North.

Following a repeat order for four further Metroriders, numbered 60-63 which arrived in March 1989, it was unfortunate that Rossendale was unsuccessful when services 441 and 442 were re-tendered and they passed to Bu-Val from 4th March. The four Metroriders were, instead, used for the 4th April start of new GMPTE contracted services 476 and 486 each operated every hour between Tottington (476) or Ainsworth (486) and Cheetham Hill via Radcliffe, Whitefield, Prestwich and North Manchester General Hospital. This major expansion of the Rossendale operating area brought them nearer to the regional centre of Manchester and was to prove a springboard for the final thrust into Manchester just one year later. April 1989 also saw the arrival of three Dominant bus-bodied Leopards from National Welsh.

Ribble's Burnley depot closed on 3rd April 1989 and, thereafter, their 273 journeys were operated from Bolton depot. From 30th May service 446 was diverted to serve Healey Corner, following withdrawal of GM Buses service 447.

11th September 1989 saw the introduction of a GM Buses competing Monday to Saturday daytime service timed just 5 minutes in front of Rossendale services 451 and 452 between Rochdale and Milnrow. In retaliation, from 9th October, Rossendale introduced competitive Monday to Saturday evening services against GM Buses on services 181 between Rochdale and Newhey and 409 between Rochdale and Oldham.

More buses joined the fleet at the end of the following month, when a batch of six Atlanteans with East Lancs bodies arrived from Eastbourne Buses' Hastings 'Topline' operation. The four older vehicles were to the long-wheelbase specification and at 82 seats were the highest capacity buses ever operated. The first secondhand Metroriders had arrived in August and this was to be repeated over the next few years as Rossendale built up a large fleet of this vehicle type.

1990 saw the purchase of more vehicles for the rapidly expanding Rossendale Coach Hire fleet. Three Tigers, fitted with Plaxton Paramount 3200 bodies, were acquired from Kentish Bus. These were soon followed by four former GM Buses Atlanteans with the standard Northern Counties body, and in August two former Ambassador Travel ECW Leyland Leopards arrived, painted in National Express livery, for use on both bus and coach work.

Within the Rochdale area, starting on 26th February, Rossendale introduced an additional 30 minute service on Mondays to Fridays between Shawforth and Rochdale, followed by further changes in June which increased services 431 and 432 to operate every 30 minutes and doubled the number of buses between Rochdale and Milnrow. However, the greatest expansion occurred from 3rd September when the Shawforth to Rochdale journeys were extended to Manchester via Middleton and Blackley, to form a new 30 minute Monday to Saturday daytime service, numbered 17. Manchester had been reached!

At the same time hourly services were introduced between Rochdale and Shore (service 454) or Stansfield (service 457). To control these extended operations, an office was opened on Rochdale Bus Station from 9th April and from September, Rossendale established its own depot in Corporation Road, Rochdale. The pattern was changing in that, whereas there had been a threat in 1986 from GM Buses wanting to operate in the Rossendale area, the situation was now reversed and Rossendale was now expanding into the GM Buses area.

In the Bury area, a new GMPTE contracted hourly Monday to Saturday daytime service was started on 2nd April, numbered 480 and operating between Bury and Ramsbottom via Lower Woodhill, Holcombe Brook and Tanners. To enable meal breaks on service 476 and 486 to be taken at

Bury Interchange, two new services, each competing with GM Buses, were introduced; 481 every hour between Tottington and Bury and 509 every hour between Ainsworth and Bury.

The year 1991 opened with the acquisition of Ellen Smith, the well known and respected coach operator based in Rochdale. The former Ellen Smith Wardleworth garage was not purchased but, instead, coaches were now based at the Rossendale Transport premises in Corporation Road. This acquisition was a pinnacle in Rossendale Transport's history and increased the total coach fleet to over thirty vehicles. Rossendale Coach Hire was gradually integrated into the Ellen Smith operations. Because of this, the rest of this history will confine itself to Rossendale Transport's bus operations and coach operations will form the basis of a separate future publication.

GMPTE tender awards from 2nd April saw Rossendale replace GM Buses on evening and Sunday services 434 (Rochdale to Turf Hill via Belfield), 438 (Rochdale to Lane Head) and 469 (hourly between Rochdale and Bury). Commercial Monday to Saturday daytime journeys were also introduced on service 439 operating every hour between Rochdale and Lane Head.

The age of the minibus was followed by the age of the midibus as some operators had a need for a vehicle which was larger than a minibus but smaller and lighter than a full size heavyweight single-decker. Dennis developed its Dart model for this purpose and met with considerable success with orders from small private operators through to the London companies. The Dart was to figure significantly in the Rossendale bus fleet of the future and the first three examples arrived in 1990. They carried Dartline bodies, designed and built by Duple before bodywork production transferred to Carlyle following the demise of Duple. They were followed in 1991 by two further examples but these carried bodies by Reeve Burgess, a subsidiary of Plaxton.

In parallel, more secondhand Metroriders arrived and on the double-deck front, nine dual door Atlanteans arrived from South Yorkshire Mainline but were converted to single door configuration before entry into service.

Technology was now moving very quickly and the Almex electronic ticket machines, purchased

Number 99, a Leyland Tiger with Duple Dominant bus body was new to Hutchison of Overtown, Scotland, in 1983 and was purchased by Rossendale in 1988. It was operating the Helmshore Circular service in Haslingden when photographed in May 1988 with Hyndburn Leyland Atlantean No 189, in that operator's dark blue and red livery, behind on the joint service 4 to Bacup. *(RM)*

in 1984, just seven years before, were all replaced by Wayfarer 2 machines with effect from 15th March 1991.

The first Dennis Darts were used on services in the Rochdale area and also, from 4th May, on service 468 which was awarded as a GMPTE tender operating hourly between Bury and Hopwood. This service was taken over from Shearings who had also operated its very first Dennis Darts on this service.

1991-1992: Sense Prevails

During early 1991, it was announced that the Bury to Manchester rail line would close for upgrade to light rail standards. To cater for this, GMPTE drew up plans for a number of dedicated bus replacement services and it was soon evident to both local operators that their scarce resources would need to be used on such services rather than the duplication that was happening on competitive services. Consequently, discussions took place between Rossendale and GM Buses to better co-ordinate their competing services. This resulted in a new timetable for service 464 which operated every 10 minutes between Accrington and Bacup and every 15 minutes between Bacup and Rochdale. Short journeys between Shawforth or

Wallbank provided eight journeys per hour between Whitworth and Rochdale. The agreement was registered with the Office of Fair Trading and meant that GM Buses journeys now reached Accrington, although Hyndburn still only got as far as Bacup. A consequence of this was that Rossendale service 17 was truncated to operate between Rochdale and Manchester, although through fares were retained by connection with the revised 464 service.

Other OFT agreements were signed to co-ordinate the Milnrow corridor, involving services 58, 181,182 (GMB) and 451, 452 (RTL) and the Littleborough corridor (services 454 and 457).

Service withdrawals from the same date included Rossendale journeys on 409, 451 (Milnrow shorts) and 454 with GM Buses withdrawing their journeys on 440 and 453.

All these changes coincided with the introduction of rail replacement services on Monday 5th August. In order to meet these

One vehicle with two bodies. WCK 123V was a Leyland Leopard with Duple Dominant 2 body, new to Ribble in 1979, and purchased by Rossendale in 1987. The photograph below, taken in Burnley in May 1988, shows it in original condition. The opposite photograph taken in September 1992 shows the vehicle after it had been rebodied by ELCB in 1992. *(RM both)*

demands, the existing Rossendale services 476 and 486 which ran parallel with the rail line for much of their route were replaced with a 30 minute service 476 between Bury and Manchester, Cannon Street calling at all stations. The northern end of the 476 was replaced by two new Rossendale Transport services: X76 operated hourly from Tottington via Ainsworth to Radcliffe, then limited stop to Manchester via Bury Old Road and X86 operated hourly from Rawtenstall via Ramsbottom, Tottington and Radcliffe where it combined with X76 to provide a combined 30 minute service. All rail replacements operated Mondays to Saturdays as there was no Sunday train service to replace in those days.

In September 1991, Bee Line, who had earlier established a depot in Rochdale, began to take a closer look at their operations and the first casualties were services 437, 444 and 445. To cover the now unserved sections of route, Rossendale diverted alternate 431 and 432 journeys to serve Kingsway as services 444 and 445.

Faced with losses which were reputed to be the highest of any of their depots, GM Buses' Rochdale depot closed from 25th November 1991, along with other depots at Altrincham, Swinton and Tameside. Rochdale's operations were transferred to Bury, Oldham and Queens Road depots with separate rotas for the former Rochdale drivers.

February 1992 saw further withdrawals of GM Buses' service R9 to Syke and Bee Line's service 447 to Wallbank. Rossendale was already the major operator in the area and was able to introduce a new service 439 to Syke and extend its service 446 to Wallbank. This meant that all routes to the north of Rochdale, along the Whitworth Road and Shawclough Road corridors, were operated by Rossendale, albeit with a few journeys of GM Buses on co-ordinated service 464.

From 6th April 1992, GM Buses withdrew their services 433, 434 and 443 between Rochdale and Turf Hill via Belfield. This, combined with the earlier Bee Line operations along Kingsway, gave Rossendale the opportunity to consolidate operations in the area and to become the major operator in the large Turf Hill Estate. This was done by diverting existing 431 and 432 services away from Well I' th' Lane to produce new circular services 431 (outward via Sudden) and 433 (outward via Belfield), each every 30 minutes serving Turf Hill and Kingsway. Services 444 and 445 were withdrawn.

From the same date, Bee Line decided to cease their final Rochdale operations and so Rossendale took the opportunity to concentrate on routes which offered a more long-term future. Routes 438 and 439 to Lane Head were withdrawn and the bus used to augment service 468 (Bury to Hopwood)

from an hourly Monday to Friday headway to every 30 minutes. It remained hourly on Saturdays. To cover the Beeline operations to the west of Rochdale, a new 30 minute Monday to Saturday daytime service 461 was registered from Rochdale to Heywood via Greave and Bamford. Services 461 and 468 were amalgamated from 1st September to form a 30 minute service 461 between Rochdale and Bury via Greave, Bamford, Heywood and Summit.

A week later, on 13th April, wasteful duplication was avoided when Rossendale service 5, which had operated hourly between Balladen and Water via Rawtenstall, was withdrawn. Since deregulation this service had competed with the rival County Council contracted service 236, operated initially by GM Buses and later by Burnley & Pendle, but without any co-ordination between the two services. It was replaced with a 30 minute daytime service between Balladen and Water, arranged to operate around the 236 times but not to operate between Rawtenstall and Water at the times of the two-hourly service 236. Alternate journeys were numbered 35 (via Foxhill Drive) and 36 (direct).

When Metrolink opened during early 1992, passengers showed some initial loyalty to the Rossendale rail replacement services and they survived in an amended form from April 1992 although service 476 was curtailed from Manchester to its former terminal arrangements in Cheetham Hill and North Manchester General Hospital. Further changes progressively reduced buses on routes 476, X76 and X86 until, from September 1994, the only remnant was an hourly service 486 between Bury and Rawtenstall via Radcliffe, Ainsworth, Tottington and Ramsbottom.

Further vehicle purchases in 1992 included more secondhand Metroriders and two Dodge minibuses which came indirectly from the GM Buses fleet. More significant though, was the decision to rebody some of the Company's Leyland Leopards with brand new EL2000 bus bodies produced by East Lancs. Whilst using old chassis did not allow for these vehicles to have as long a life as brand new vehicles, their cost was less than half that of a new vehicle and nine such East Lancs rebuilds, numbered 70, 71, 73-79 were acquired

Rochdale town centre is the setting for this view of Atlantean No. 136 operating local service 440 from Rochdale to Syke on Mayday 1990. It was one of six purchased from Hastings Top Line in 1989. *(RM)*

over the next few years, including some which had received their new bodies with previous operators before joining the Rossendale fleet.

As Rossendale Transport services from the Bury direction into Manchester were reducing, there was a marked increase in popularity of service 17 operating between Rochdale and Manchester. Drivers were reporting feedback from passengers that GM Buses regularly failed to materialise throughout the day. It was evident that the greater reliability of the Rossendale service was building up a passenger loyalty that demanded buses throughout the day and so it was decided to introduce a 30 minute evening service on the route from 23rd November 1992.

Rossendale's service 480 was replaced in March 1993 by new service 476 operating between Bury and Peel Brow via Woodhill, Tanners and Ramsbottom. This resulted in a further OFT agreement being signed in order to co-ordinate services through Woodhill to provide an even 15 minute headway. The other services concerned were 475 (operated by Burnley & Pendle trading as Whizzard) and 477 (operated by both GM Buses and Rossendale). From June, service 476 was extended to Edenfield.

The battles with GM Buses had now ended, although there was still heated competition on certain routes. In order to expand, Rossendale needed to look elsewhere and GMPTE tenders were examined as a springboard for further operations. Successes over the next few years included services 96 (Manchester to Simister), 97 and 98 (Manchester to Bury), 124 (Rochdale to Manchester), 134 (Manchester to Middleton), 159 (Middleton to Oldham via Failsworth and Woodhouses), 164 (Rochdale to Manchester via Darn Hill), 403 (Shaw Circulars), 406 (Middleton to Oldham) and 408 (Shaw to Stalybridge via Oldham). This expansion of the operating area was later to prove disastrous as the company's training, engineering and supervisory resources were stretched ever further afield.

The year 1993 was one of consolidation and no major changes were made to commercial services. Vehicle acquisitions saw the arrival of two used Leyland Olympians from Stevensons of Uttoxeter and a Volvo Citybus from Wrights of Wrexham, all three having bodies by East Lancashire Coachbuilders. The Olympians, which had been new to Eastbourne, received a 'Valley Link' livery

for operation on the express services X76 and X86 operated between Rawtenstall and Manchester. There were, of course, more used Metroriders entering the fleet, this year's intake being five from Liverbus and one from Yorkshire Rider.

Whilst Rossendale began to experience corrosion problems with the MCW Metroriders, it was still very satisfied with the concept of the vehicle and so decided to purchase two more new Metroriders, but to a higher build specification introduced by Optare of Leeds which had taken over the manufacturing rights from MCW. Rossendale purchased two examples of the Optare model in each of the years 1993, 1994 and 1997.

Rossendale buses had been operating empty mileage between Rawtenstall and Rochdale since 1986 in order to get buses to/from the Rochdale operations. Whilst frequent buses operated on service 464 between the two towns, the most direct route was via Owd Betts, a route that could trace its ancestry back to the Ribble and Scout Motor Services route 244 between Rochdale and Blackpool via Blackburn and Preston. At deregulation, the route had been advertised for tender by Lancashire County Council but was considered to be commercial by GM Buses who needed a route to reach their contracted operations in Rossendale and Blackburn. Following the demise of those operations the route was deregistered by GM Buses and from February 1988 was operated as service 240 by Burnley & Pendle on contract to Lancashire, and in conjunction with the other trunk route 236 between Burnley and Blackburn via Water and Rawtenstall. From 1st May 1994 Rossendale were successful in being awarded route 240 on a two hourly daily basis between Rochdale and Rawtenstall.

The same date saw the termination of the Lancashire contract, which Burnley & Pendle operated between Burnley, Water, Rawtenstall and Blackburn as service 236. Since 13th April 1993, Rossendale had operated a Monday to Friday peak hour journey on the route and now decided to infill with a two hourly Monday to Friday commercial service between Rawtenstall and Blackburn. These journeys were linked with the service 36 journeys between Water and Rawtenstall to form a through service. Burnley & Pendle decided to retain its Burnley to Blackburn journeys on a commercial basis: every two hours on Monday to Friday and hourly on Saturdays. As a consequence, service

35 continued as an hourly service between Balladen and Water via Foxhill Drive (intertimed with service 236 journeys) and service 36 became confined to an hourly Rawtenstall to Balladen service (intertimed with service 35).

1993-1996: The Period of Bus Company Purchases

Following claims that GM Buses was too large and therefore had an unfair monopoly, the Government decreed that the company be split into two halves with effect from 13th December 1993. Known as GM Buses North and GM Buses South, both new companies were sold to their respective employees following a bidding process. Stagecoach had been one of the unsuccessful bidders for GM Buses South and so decided that its subsidiary company, Ribble, should register a 10 minute service on the prime route between Manchester and Stockport from 31st January 1994. In retaliation, GM Buses South used their Charterplan subsidiary to begin operating every 30 minutes on service X43 Manchester to Nelson, which was reputed to be the most profitable route operated by Stagecoach (Ribble).

Not only did the number of vehicles on the route double, but fares were slashed by both companies as they fought for market share. This had an adverse effect on Rossendale's service 273 journeys between Rawtenstall and Burnley where

fares had to be lowered to less than half of the previous levels. The battle continued for over a year and it is only now, in the year 2007, that fare levels have returned to the same scale as other services.

The 1994 intake of vehicles comprised Optare Metroriders (13 and 14) and two new Volvo Olympian double-deckers with Alexander Royale bodies, which were the first Rossendale vehicles to be fitted with kneeling devices to aid boarding.

Since deregulation, GM Buses and Rossendale had each operated an hourly bus to provide a combined 30 minute service on service 435 (Rochdale to Buckstones). It was obvious to everyone that the Rossendale journeys were better supported by passengers and it came as no surprise when GM Buses North announced that they would withdraw their journeys after 4th November 1994. So it was that Rossendale became the sole operator of a 30 minute headway from 6th November 1994.

To enable this to happen, service 456 (Rochdale to Littleborough) was withdrawn from the same date and service 446 was truncated to form two new circular services, 445 and 446, serving the various estate roads in the Shawclough area.

XPW 876X, a Leyland Leopard with a dual-purpose express body by Eastern Coach Works, was an unusual vehicle to find in a municipal fleet, having been designed mainly for National Express operation. It dated from 1982 and was purchased from Ambassador Travel in 1990. In August 1992 it was seen taking on passengers in Bolton for service X69 to Fleetwood. *(RM)*

Wallbank remained served by jointly operated service 467 via Whitworth Road.

Another withdrawal by GM Buses North at this time was the evening and Sunday service 469 journeys between Tottington and Jericho, which were registered commercially by Rossendale and linked with the existing Bury to Rochdale contracted journeys with effect from 6th November 1994.

Following the withdrawal of the GM Buses South journeys on X43 from 4th February 1995, Ribble decided to look closely at its operations in the area and decided that economies could be made by reducing the duplication of services between Burnley and Rawtenstall. Consequently, from 7th May 1995, evening and Sunday journeys on service 273 were curtailed to only operate between Bolton and Rawtenstall with onward connections to/from Burnley using service 743. These journeys were all operated by Rossendale, but from 22nd June 1997 every alternate journey (two hourly) was diverted as service 473 via Edgworth to replace service 563.

A revolutionary new Dial-A-Ride service, numbered 20, started on 28th June 1995, albeit only on Tuesday and Friday each week. This was made possible by the rescheduling of local minibus services 8, 10, 15 and 17 which meant that a bus was available for the new service except on Wednesday, Thursday and Saturday when it was required to operate the Bacup local services. A special vehicle, fitted with wheelchair lift, was required to operate these services and a Talbot Freeway, numbered 199, was the chosen vehicle. Monday was scheduled for regular maintenance. Other deliveries in 1995 were nine secondhand Metroriders from Blackburn Transport, Rhondda and Sovereign.

Perhaps the biggest change to services in Rochdale came late in 1995 when GM Buses North gave notice that they were to withdraw from services to the west of Rochdale, except for the trunk routes 469 and 471 towards Bury. In the preceding months, Rossendale had been facing increased GM Buses duplication on service 17 and this, in turn, had increased reliability and hence public confidence in the GM Buses route. Problems of recruitment and supervising services further away from depot meant that Rossendale made a momentous decision to withdraw service 17 and instead use Rossendale's resources closer

Two new Volvo Olympians with Alexander Royale bodies joined the fleet in 1994, and one of these, No. 29, was passing through Rawtenstall in October 1994 on the mainline service 464 to Accrington when it was caught by the camera. *(RM)*

to home, to operate services towards Norden which had been withdrawn by GM Buses North. Another advantage was that these services could have synergy with the existing service 240 operating between Rochdale and Rawtenstall via Norden. As a result, from 23rd October 1995, services 17 (Rochdale to Manchester) and 457 (Rochdale to Littleborough) were withdrawn and replaced by services 443 (Rochdale to Elmsfield), 444 (Rochdale to Norden Mill Bridge), 445 (Rochdale to Shawfield) and 461 (Rochdale to Bury via Bamford and Heywood) each operating every 30 minutes to produce a co-ordinated 8 journeys per hour towards Norden.

From 11th December 1995, service 240 reverted to its original number of 244 and the 444 journeys were integrated to form a 30 minute service to Norden (Norden Way) with a two hourly extension (subsidised by Lancashire County Council) to Rawtenstall.

1996 opened with a number of potential threats for Rossendale Transport.

In the south of its operating territory First Group was successful in its bid for GM Buses North but gave assurances to Rossendale Transport that the newly found concordat would continue.

In east Lancashire, however, matters seemed to be deteriorating when on 31st January, Pendle Borough Council agreed to sell its 50% shareholding of Burnley & Pendle to Stagecoach. Despite much local unrest, representations to the Office of Fair Trading proved fruitless and the sale went ahead from 1st April 1996, followed by the subsequent sale of the remaining 50% shareholding held by Burnley Council on 7th March 1997.

Whilst Rossendale Transport did not have any joint operations with Burnley & Pendle, its neighbouring local authority bus company in Hyndburn was involved in the operation of service 464 and on 21st May, Hyndburn Borough Council formally resolved to sell Hyndburn Transport. At the same time it was discovered that Hyndburn Transport had registered commercial school journeys in Rochdale to commence the following September.

Matters moved swiftly and on 12th June, a letter was sent from Rossendale Transport to the Chief Executive of Hyndburn Council telling him of the company's concerns about any new owner becoming a joint operator on service 464. Service 464 was registered with the Traffic Commissioner in the name of Rossendale Transport Limited but also included journeys operated by the other joint operators, GM Buses and Hyndburn. It was pointed out that Rossendale had a legal obligation to ensure that all journeys operated in accordance with the registered particulars.

An assurance was requested that any subsequent purchaser would continue to operate those journeys but no reply was received by 17th July when an announcement was made by Hyndburn Borough Council that talks had collapsed with the preferred bidder, which had earlier been named as Blackpool Transport Services Ltd.

On the same evening, board members of Rossendale Transport agreed to a number of calculated measures, which would take effect from the following Monday, if assurances could not be given. So it was that on the morning of Monday 22nd July, Hyndburn drivers reported to work only to find all their journeys were being operated by Rossendale Transport. A letter delivered at 06.00 hours to Hyndburn's Managing Director stated 'With effect from commencement of services today, Monday 22nd July 1996, Rossendale Transport has made arrangements to cover all journeys currently allocated to and operated by Hyndburn Transport. You therefore no longer have any legal obligation to operate any journeys with effect from today's date. I will arrange for the name of Hyndburn Transport to be deleted from the registration with effect from Monday 9th September which will allow you 42 days' notice to register your own existing journeys should you so wish'.

To say that Hyndburn employees were annoyed would be an understatement and the local newspapers carried accusations and counter accusations for days on end as the 'bus war' developed. Blackpool's withdrawal from the proposed sale now created a vacuum and ironically, Rossendale Transport was approached to make a bid without having to sign the normal disclosure agreement which would have precluded it from any competition with Hyndburn.

The announcement that Rossendale Transport was now the preferred bidder caused further resentment amongst the Hyndburn workforce and, whilst Rossendale did make a bid, it took into account the unprofitability of most routes and nowhere near matched the Stagecoach valuation of over five million pounds made for the Burnley

& Pendle undertaking, and on which the Council had set their expectations.

On 9th August, Hyndburn Council announced that an offer had been received from another bidder and by 27th September, Stagecoach was confirmed as the successful purchaser. Consequently, the three contested vehicle workings reverted to Stagecoach operation, but Rossendale Rover tickets continued to be accepted on their vehicles.

1996 –2002: Quality v Quantity

Whilst these various ownership issues were resolved, discussions continued with Greater Manchester PTE, which was willing to 'kick-start' the use of low floor accessible vehicles within the County by providing funding towards the purchase of suitable vehicles. The local services within Bury were chosen as the test bed for Rossendale Transport and it was agreed to purchase 5 Dennis Dart SLF vehicles with the new 9.0 metre long, 2.4 metre wide Spryte body being built by East Lancs Coachbuilders. At the time these were the first small low floor buses to be built to the new GMPTE vehicle specification that eventually became the Disability Discrimination Act specification in the year 2000. Many alterations were made to ensure the manoeuvrability of wheelchairs within such a narrow vehicle and the

various filled holes in the floor of bus 106 are testimony to this.

The vehicles sported a new EASYRIDE livery designed by Ken Mortimer, the former design officer of Greater Manchester Transport. Along the cantrail, buses proclaimed their advantages such as 'Low Floor Bus', 'Easy Access' and 'Low Emission Engine' and incorporated a swept down rainbow effect to accentuate the kneeling facility provided on these buses. They were some of the first East Lancs buses to incorporate the new Alusuisse method of construction and so were claimed to be 'locally built to a brand new design, featuring new safety construction, air suspension and modern seating to give maximum comfort'. These claims were not unfounded and in 2007 they still provide sterling service in the Bury area. From 22nd July 1996 these buses were used on local services between Bury and Norden (479, 480), Chesham (492), Fern Grove (494) and Limefield (499). Subsequently, another three similar vehicles were delivered in Spring 1997 for use on service 435 (Rochdale to Buckstones).

Other vehicle purchases in 1996 consisted of three Atlanteans with Northern Counties bodies from GM Buses South and a further three Metroriders from Rhondda.

As mentioned earlier, operation of contracted services on behalf of GMPTE had been growing in outlying areas and in particular GMPTE were concerned about the reliability and performance of Rossendale's service 159 between Middleton and Oldham. In the Bury area, similar concerns were being expressed about the operation of Bluebird's service 465 to Heywood and

Number 188 was one of eight Leyland Atlanteans with Alexander bodies dating from 1981, and purchased from South Yorkshire PTE in 1991. It is shown in Rochdale heading for Accrington in April 1997, and was withdrawn in 1998. *(MB)*

so it was that from September 1996, GMPTE reassigned the contracts so that Rossendale lost service 159 but gained the 465 operation. From 5th October GM Buses withdrew the off-peak journeys between Bury and Nangreaves, only to be replaced by GMPTE subsidised service 498 operated by Rossendale. From 20th April 1998 both services were combined with service 492 to produce an hourly through service from Nangreaves via Chesham, Bury and Fairfield to Heywood.

A further threat in 1996 was the formation of MR Travel, a new bus company set up by Mike Royds who had been the manager of the former Bee Line operations in Rochdale. Unfortunately for Rossendale Transport, Mike lived in Whitworth in the heart of Rossendale's service 464 route. For a number of years, from the spring of 1996, he persevered with the operation of a new service 465 between Rochdale and Shawforth, which had a regular passenger following. For a period of time from December 1996 to March 1997 he also operated service 533 between Syke, Rochdale, Belfield and Turf Hill as a competing service with two of Rossendale's local services but this proved uneconomic and he settled down to providing the 30 minute 465 service. In September 2000, he decided to withdraw his buses from the Knowsley Crescent estate in Shawforth and Ellen Smith (Tours) operated a short-lived service over the winter to serve the estate. This resulted in a complaint by Mike Royds to the Office of Fair Trading which found in favour of Ellen Smith. Early in 2004, it was announced that the bus operations of MR Travel were to be purchased by Bluebird and the final MR Travel journeys on service 465 ceased after operation on 27th March 2004.

Stagecoach (Ribble) took full control of Burnley & Pendle from 7th March 1997 and very soon thereafter, the operation of service 475 (Bury to Ramsbottom) was transferred to Ribble's Bolton depot. The operation was divorced from the main Bolton operations and regularly suffered from missing journeys so that Ribble deregistered the service and Rossendale Transport commenced operation on 16th November 1998.

During 1997 two more Metroriders (15 and 16) became the last new purchases of this type. Secondhand purchases saw another four Atlanteans (the last of this type to join the fleet)

from Stagecoach Manchester and two Volvo B10Ms with Duple 300 bus bodies from Hutchison of Overtown. The most significant purchase, however, was of sixteen Dennis Darts with 8.5 m long Carlyle Dartline bodies. These came from London operator Metroline Travel, but were shorter than the similar buses purchased new in 1991. This meant that they could be used on routes where only Metroriders could be used beforehand. They were an immediate success with both drivers and passengers who perceived them as a 'real' bus rather than a minibus.

Whilst Rossendale Transport had taken delivery of a small number of new minibuses and single-deck buses in the period since 1986, it was becoming increasingly obvious that the age profile of the fleet was worsening by the day. In particular the main route through Rawtenstall, service 464, was operated by a collection of double-deckers, some bought new by Rossendale Borough Transport but many being secondhand vehicles that had been purchased to mount competitive responses in more recent years. Given that competition with major operators had now ceased, a decision was made to order the largest batch of new buses purchased by Rossendale Transport or any of its predecessors since the 1949 all-Leyland PD2s for Rawtenstall. These ten Dennis Dart buses were to be used on service 464 but unlike previous Darts they were to be the new 11.3 metre long Super Darts equipped with the larger Allison World Series gearbox and fitted with Super Pointer bodies by Plaxton. New high quality publicity was prepared to reflect the branding of 'Mainline 464' carried on the vehicles.

However, at the same time, the potential of this service attracted the attentions of Pilkingtons of Accrington which initially registered journeys between Accrington and Haslingden commencing in February 1998 and later as far as Bacup. Worse was to come for, in October, they started a 30 minute headway service between Accrington and Bacup, built around school tenders they had been awarded in the Rossendale area. Fares were below those charged by the established operators and initially Rossendale matched the Pilkington journeys and fares by providing additional journeys numbered A2B operated mainly by Metroriders. This was made possible by registering a frequent interval service between Accrington and Bacup so that all journeys on service A2B and the 464 journeys operated by Rossendale, First and Stagecoach could be operated flexibly as long as a minimum 10 minute headway was maintained.

The quandary however was whether to cancel the order for the new Darts. Convinced there would be considerable savings in engineering costs compared to the ageing Atlanteans, the order was confirmed and from 2nd November 1998, the ten new Dennis Super Pointer Darts were introduced in a blaze of publicity, including the invitation, carried on each bus, to 'Leave the car at home and join us on the Ultimate Travel Experience.' It soon became apparent that passengers were supporting these new buses and a decision was made to withdraw the additional Metrorider journeys and to compete on quality rather than quantity. Dedicated drivers were used on the 'Mainline 464' service and they were all specially trained in customer care and disability awareness, facets which were thought to be revolutionary at the time but which are now accepted as normal within public transport.

Pilkingtons continued their operation, initially with Leyland Nationals but later using an assortment of Optare Deltas, Leyland National 'Greenway' rebuilds and the occasional double-decker, until, following a Public Inquiry, the Traffic Commissioner terminated all Pilkington registrations with effect from 23rd July 2004. In reality, their services between Accrington and Bacup ceased two weeks prior to this date as drivers left the company to find employment elsewhere.

Whilst the new Dart SPDs replaced many of the double-deckers on service 464, the company was facing increasing attention from Ministry of Transport vehicle inspectors with regard to oil leaks on Atlanteans and so further withdrawals took place when an opportunity arose to purchase a batch of ten Olympians. These came from London Central as ECW bodied dual door vehicles and many of them actually entered service in this condition, but were quickly converted to single door layout before the end of the year. Many of the original MCW Metroriders were now suffering from corrosion problems and a further batch of six short Carlyle Darts was acquired from Metroline Travel to enable disposal of the worst examples. Four longer Darts, this time with the Dartline-derived body built by Marshall of Cambridge arrived from Maynes of Manchester in early 1999.

The only developments during early 1999 were to the more rural services: From 17th January a new Sunday and Bank Holiday service 50 was introduced between Rawtenstall East Lancashire Railway Station and Todmorden via Bacup. It operated approximately every two hours and was funded by the government's rural bus initiative. By contrast, 24th October was the last day of operation of Sunday service 244 between Rawtenstall and Rochdale via Owd Betts. How ironic that government money could be used to subsidise new rural services without a proven demand but could not be used towards long-established routes such as 244. In the event, service 50 soldiered on until it was withdrawn on 10th April 2006, following the withdrawal of support.

To replace older Metroriders, four more recent examples were acquired from APCOA and five further Olympians arrived from London United although this time they were already single-doored and did not require conversion. Although outwardly similar to the ECW body, these had been built at Leyland's Workington plant.

Following a decision by Stagecoach (Ribble) to withdraw the former Burnley & Pendle route 236 between Burnley and Blackburn via Rawtenstall, Rossendale Transport decided to register an hourly Monday to Saturday daytime service between Water and Blackburn with effect from 24th October 1999. Lancashire County Council provided support for extensions from Water to Burnley operating every two hours Monday to Friday but hourly on Saturdays. Ironically, Lancashire decided at the same time that the Water to Burnley section was no longer required during the week, Monday to Friday, but journeys continued to be provided until their withdrawal on Christmas Eve. Subsidy continued from 4th January 2000 for the Saturday extensions, which were comparatively well used for shopping journeys to Burnley.

At the end of 1999, Stagecoach (Ribble) decided to relaunch its X43 Manchester service, with increased frequencies. As it had done with the evening and Sunday journeys back in 1995, Ribble now decided that, with effect from 4th January 2000, it would withdraw weekday service 273 between Burnley and Rawtenstall. The remaining hourly 273 journeys between Rawtenstall and Bolton were all to be operated by Rossendale Transport who also retained their existing separate hourly service between Rawtenstall and Burnley but now numbered 243 to avoid confusion.

Another surprise at this time was that First Manchester, the successor to GM Buses, being faced with staff recruitment problems and the need to familiarise all staff to Accrington, gave notice to withdraw from service 464 with effect from 26th February 2000. Obviously, Rossendale agreed to cover these journeys but was faced with the predicament that the public now expected all Rossendale buses to be EASYRIDE low floor standard. It was necessary, therefore, to hire three low floor buses from Dawson Rentals to cover work from 28th February. These were also Plaxton bodied Dart SLFs and ran in allover white livery with EASYRIDE fleet names applied. A repeat order was placed for an additional four new Plaxton Super Pointer Darts, identical to the initial ten vehicles, and these eventually arrived at the end of September to replace the hired vehicles.

Only Rossendale and Stagecoach (Ribble) remained as joint operators on service 464, competing with Pilkingtons. In order to remove the anomaly that former Hyndburn journeys had never operated beyond Bacup to Rochdale, the timetable was revised from 16th July 2000 and Ribble vehicles now regularly ran into Rochdale Bus Station.

Whilst the number of journeys between Rawtenstall and Burnley had been increased by relaunched service X43 from January, Ribble had not increased the number of stops on that section of route, despite having withdrawn its own 273 stopping service. Only the Rossendale hourly 243 journeys remained to serve all stops and so from 4th September service 243 was increased to operate every 30 minutes Monday to Saturday daytime.

The contract for the Saturday journey extensions of service 236 from Water to Burnley expired on Saturday 14th October 2000 and tenders were invited for a replacement. The successful bidder was Northern Blue which decided to extend its service 88, with effect from 21st October, to provide an hourly Saturday service between Burnley General Hospital, Burnley, Water, Rawtenstall and Rossendale Hospital.

Vehicle purchases in 2000 consisted of ten dual-doored Leyland Lynx, for use on normal service work and school contracts. These came from

Lothian and necessitated conversion to single door layout before entry into service. An ex-Harrogate & District Mercedes Benz minibus was hired and numbered 198, for use on service 465 competing with MR Travel between Rochdale and Shawforth. A similar vehicle, but fitted with tail-lift, was purchased from Arriva to replace the Talbot Freeway which had been used on CountyRider services since 1995. This was given fleet number 199 like its predecessor.

To capitalise on Rossendale's new found monopoly on service 273, journeys were doubled to produce a 30 minute Monday to Saturday headway with effect from 10th January 2001.

From 26th February, rather than operating 30 minute headways on routes 439 and 440 between Rochdale and Syke, service 439 was withdrawn and a 15 minute service provided on service 440 so that more buses served Rochdale Infirmary. To cater for the section of route along Bentley Street, which had been served by the 439, alternate service 446 journeys were diverted and became route 447.

On 15th April 2001 came the staggering news that Blazefield Holdings had purchased the Stagecoach (Ribble) operations carried out from depots at Blackburn, Bolton, Burnley and Clitheroe. Operations at Blackburn, Bolton and Clitheroe were renamed Lancashire United Travel Limited whilst Burnley depot became Burnley and Pendle Travel Limited. With this development, Lancashire United replaced Ribble as the joint operator of service 464.

The 21st April was the last day of operation of Blackburn Transport's service 703 which had operated between Blackburn, Accrington and Bury since deregulation in October 1986. This meant that there was no longer a link between Accrington and Haslingden into Bury, but more importantly the village of Ewood Bridge now found itself without any regular bus service. Consequently, Lancashire County Council awarded a contract to Rossendale Transport to provide new service 482 operating two return journeys per day, Monday to Friday, between Accrington and Bury via Ewood Bridge.

One of Shearings' best performing routes at its Bolton depot had been service 508 which operated between Bury and Bolton via Greenmount and Affetside. Once taken over by GM Buses it failed to meet their financial targets and was deregistered. Blue Bus took on the service but again, was unable to make the service a commercial proposition.

It was from 3rd September that Rossendale commenced operation of an hourly Monday to Saturday daytime service 508 with financial assistance from GMPTE to retain operation via Affetside. The remainder of the route was considered commercial, particularly as it was to operate on the opposite half hour to the original hourly service 273, and therefore replaced the additional 273 journeys that had operated since January 2001.

Discussions with East Lancs Coachbuilders revealed that they would shortly be allowed to body the higher specification SPD version of the Dart. In the meantime, they were able to offer, for immediate delivery, an East Lancs body on a six cylinder Dart SLF which was in construction but had been cancelled by Bluebird of Moston. This vehicle, numbered 135, was the first Rossendale vehicle to receive a new style registration mark using a system of numbers to denote the period of registration, as opposed to prefix or suffix letters that had been used since 1963. Delivered in September 2001, number 135 was fitted with the blue moquette that was standard at Bluebird. Five similar Spryte SLF vehicles with blue moquette arrived in January 2002 to complete the order, but these were fitted with 4 cylinder Euro 3 engines.

The only other vehicles purchased during 2001 were two ex-Brighton Leyland Lynx which spent most of their lives operating school journeys from Rochdale depot.

The end of 2001 saw the rerouting of First Bus route 509 to operate via Walshaw as route 510 with the intention of withdrawing their service 481

between Bury and Holcombe Brook via Walshaw. Once again, this was an opportunity for Rossendale to utilise its existing services to fill the gap left by a First Bus withdrawal. Rossendale registered an hourly Monday to Saturday daytime service 481 between Bury and Holcombe Brook with service 508 amended to operate on the opposite half hour between Bury and Holcombe via Walshaw.

During July 2002, Manchester was host to the Commonwealth Games and Rossendale was one of many operators who provided Park & Ride services between Heaton Park and Sport City, the newly built stadium which was subsequently to become the home for Manchester City Football Club.

To operate these services, Rossendale ordered a batch of eight Dennis Dart SPD chassis to be bodied with the new East Lancs SPD Spryte body but delivery delays meant that only two vehicles arrived in time for use on the Park & Ride services. These were the first UK vehicles to be fitted with the new Mobitec destination equipment and everyone was amazed that they could be seen at such great distances. They were also the newest buses to be used to serve this major sporting event. The remaining six vehicles did not materialise until September but at least that meant they were fitted with the later '52' registration plates. All eight were then allocated to service 464 which allowed some of the original Plaxton SPDs to be cascaded to other routes.

The Wayfarer 2 ticket machines purchased in 1991 had more than exceeded the life of their predecessors but by this time were beginning to give trouble. Wayfarer now produced a new

Number 139 was one of six Dennis Dart SLF low floor models which were purchased in 2000/1 and carrying ELCB bodies. In August 2003 it was operating in Bury on service 483 to Rawtenstall and Water. (MB)

generation machine which was able to provide much better trip data and incorporated global positioning technology (GPS) which automatically updated the boarding point information. The introduction of this new technology had to be carefully timed, between the conclusion of the Commonwealth Games and the school resumption dates, and so was implemented from Sunday 11th August.

Other vehicle purchases in 2002 consisted of a batch of four Dart SLFs with Plaxton Pointer bodywork which were purchased from Blue Bus of Horwich.

2002-2007: Provision of New Links

The local hospital at Bury General, situated on service 483, closed in 2002 and most facilities were moved to Bury Fairfield which, although served by Rossendale buses, did not have a direct bus into Lancashire. From 1st September 2002, service 479 was truncated to operate between Bury and Limefield only. The section of route between Fairfield and Bury was linked with service 483 (Bury to Rawtenstall) and services 36 and 236 between Rawtenstall and Water to form a new 30 minute Monday to Saturday daytime low floor route between Fairfield and Water. This reinstated the former service which ran between Bury and Water prior to the 1982 route changes. At the same time an additional hourly commercial service 483 was introduced between Bury and Rawtenstall during the daytime on Sundays. The opposite end of route 36, the section of route between Rawtenstall and Balladen, was now served by a new Monday to Saturday daytime service 1 operating every 30 minutes.

There was therefore no longer a need for service 236 (Blackburn to Water) to serve the Rawtenstall to Water section and so the Blackburn to Rawtenstall section was linked with service 244 to provide an improved Monday to Saturday hourly service 244 from Blackburn to Rochdale via Rawtenstall. At first Foxhill Drive was left unserved but from 2nd December, three return journeys were provided on Mondays and Thursdays by a new service 9, operated by Rossendale Transport on behalf of Lancashire County Council. At this time Lancashire County tried to persuade Northern Blue to divert its Saturday 88 journeys via Foxhill Drive but to no avail.

Services 32, 33 and 34 had survived virtually unchanged since their creation at deregulation. Close examination showed, however, that the central part of the route between Edgeside and Bacup was very poorly used and the service was truncated to operate in two sections. During the daytime, Mondays to Saturdays, service 3 was to operate every 30 minutes between Rawtenstall and Edgeside, whereas service 47 was to provide a two hourly service between Todmorden and Burnley via Bacup. Hourly contracted services were provided evenings and Sundays on service 1 (Rawtenstall to Balladen), service 3 (Rawtenstall to Edgeside) and service 483 (Rawtenstall to Water via Newchurch). The comparatively few passengers who had previously used services 33 and 34 along Booth Road and New Line were advised to use the CountyRider service.

Whilst the September changes were welcomed by the public, especially the new cross-Rawtenstall facilities to Bury Fairfield Hospital, First Bus took exception to the new facilities and consequently, from 30th September, extended their Monday to Saturday service 90 (Rawtenstall to Manchester via Brandlesholme and Bury) to provide a 30 minute service to and from Accrington. Unfortunately there were few staff still at their Bury depot who remembered the 464 route to Accrington and so every journey had to be accompanied by a trainer between Rawtenstall and Accrington. Obviously such an expensive operation could not be sustained and the service reverted to its Rawtenstall terminus from 27th January 2003.

At the end of 2002, Rossendale experienced severe staff shortages and so asked Burnley & Pendle if they could operate the journeys on service 47 (Burnley to Todmorden) and 243 (Rawtenstall to Burnley) whilst staffing problems were resolved. As service 47 came no closer to Rawtenstall than Bacup, it was an obvious choice for transfer as it could be operated by Blazefield from Burnley. This transfer took effect from 9th December, but Blazefield astounded Rossendale by announcing its intention for Lancashire United to withdraw from service 464 after 25th January. Obviously, this was another opportunity not to be missed and it was agreed to take on the additional journeys from 27th January 2003, but with an existing staffing problem there was a need to transfer some other work to another operator until such time as staffing levels improved. Only Burnley & Pendle had the resources to cover additional work and the only Rossendale route known to them was service 273. From 24th February, Burnley & Pendle took over Rossendale's service 273 (Rawtenstall to Bolton) and linked it into their existing service 143 (Burnley to Rawtenstall) to once again resurrect the 273 service between Burnley and Bolton. Service 273 between Bolton and Rawtenstall eventually returned to Rossendale Transport with effect from 15th August 2005.

Another consequence of the transfer of facilities from Bury General to Fairfield was that residents along the Bury to Ramsbottom corridor could no longer reach the Hospital. As a consequence, GMPTE contracted services 476 and 480 were combined from 24th February to form a new Monday to Friday hourly daytime service 476 between Peel Brow, Tanners, Woodhill, Bury, Fairfield and Norden. Service 479 was amended to operate every hour between Limefield Brow and Topping Fold via Bury. As this freed up the service number 480, that number was subsequently used, from 28th April, when the 508 was renumbered 480 so that services 480 and 481 provided a co-ordinated timetable.

Few service changes occurred in 2003 except that, from 2nd August, Rossendale introduced an hourly subsidised service 19 between Burnley and Rawtenstall, replacing Northern Blue's service 88.

The connection to Rossendale Hospital was retained by linking service 19 with the Helmshore circulars, but the main difference was that service 19 now diverted via Foxhill Drive.

During the summer of 2003 Rossendale had on loan a Volvo B7RLE demonstrator with bodywork by Wrights of Ballymena. This resulted in the delivery of six such vehicles at the end of August 2003, followed in December by a further example plus the vehicle which had been on demonstration earlier in the year. All eight were turned out in the 'Mainline 464' livery, allowing further SPDs to be cascaded to other work. Bus number 150 of this batch became the very first Rossendale bus to be displayed by a manufacturer at a major industry exhibition, when it appeared as an official Volvo exhibit at the Coach & Bus Show held at the National Exhibition Centre in October 2003.

With effect from 25th January 2004, Blazefield (Burnley & Pendle) withdrew service 47 and extended its local service number 8 to produce an

In September 2003 eight new Volvo B7RLE models with bodies by Wrights of Ballymena, Northern Ireland, were introduced on Mainline Service 464 to replace some of the original Dennis Darts. Number 152 from this group is shown at Bacup awaiting departure to Rochdale in October 2005. *(MB)*

hourly Monday to Saturday service operating between Burnley and Bacup via Plumbe Street (where the Northern Blue depot was located) and Branch Road. As these revised journeys now showed service number 8, the remaining Rossendale Transport contracted school journeys were renumbered 48 to reflect the original route into Burnley. Operation of service 8 passed to Northern Blue with effect from 31st January 2005.

As a consequence of the deregistration of the Bacup to Todmorden section of service 47, Lancashire County Council invited tenders for an hourly Monday to Saturday daytime service 49 between Bacup and Todmorden. Rossendale Transport was successful but because of the staffing problems which still applied at Rawtenstall, it was operated by two dedicated drivers from Rochdale.

Following on from the success of service 483 which linked Bury with parts of Rossendale that had previously not had a direct service, another direct service was provided from 22nd February 2004 when a 30 minute Monday to Saturday service 482 was introduced between Bury and Edgeside via Balladen, Hall Carr, Rawtenstall and Newchurch. This allowed the withdrawal of daytime services 1 (Rawtenstall to Balladen), service 3 (Rawtenstall to Edgeside) and the short journeys on service 483 between Bury and Rawtenstall.

Evening and Sunday contracted journeys remained on services 1 and 3 as did the hourly Sunday commercial journeys on service 483. Because of the introduction of this service it was necessary to renumber the existing route between Accrington to Bury and become 484 instead of 482. From the same date, the days of operation of service 9, between Foxhill Drive and Rawtenstall, were extended to be Mondays to Fridays.

Timekeeping problems on the Rochdale to Norden corridor led to a revision to services in the area, also from 22nd February. Rather than operating via Greave, which it had done since its introduction, service 461, operating every 30 minutes, was diverted along Spotland Road to provide a co-ordinated 10 minute daytime headway with services 244, 444 and 445. Service 443 was withdrawn and Elmsfield was served by a diversion of service 461, whereas, in Heywood, the route of service 461 was amended to serve both the Summit Estate and Bury Old Road. Evening

and Sunday journeys between Heywood and Rochdale followed the old route and, accordingly, were numbered 460 to avoid confusion.

To the south of Rochdale, Monday to Saturday daytime services 431 and 433 were withdrawn and replaced by new service 434 operating every 30 minutes but covering only the Belfield end of the circle and terminating in Kirkholt Estate. Evening and Sunday journeys continued to operate between Rochdale and Castleton via Belfield, showing service number 433 in each direction. After passenger representations to GMPTE and with their financial assistance, all 434 journeys were extended from Kirkholt to Castleton with effect from 29th March 2004.

In Bury, operation of service 479 (Limefield to Topping Fold) passed from Rossendale to Ashalls but at the same time Rossendale were awarded the full operation of service 477 (Bury to Summerseat) which had previously been operated mainly by First Bus.

Following the cessation of Metrorider production by Optare, Rossendale Transport had been looking for alternative vehicle models that were of low floor design but which also could negotiate the narrow roads followed by many of its services. The most obvious choice was the Optare Solo but, at the time, it was only offered in full-width specification. Attention moved to Mercedes who had designed a low floor vehicle based on the Sprinter van chassis and bodied in Germany by Koch. Four of these vehicles were introduced to routes 465 and 476 from early March 2004, replacing Metroriders. They soon became very popular and passenger numbers grew to a point where they exceeded the vehicles' limited capacity.

Experience of operators elsewhere in the country showed that passenger growth could be generated by a simplified service pattern that gave passengers the confidence to 'turn up and go'. As discussions were taking place with Lancashire County Council to upgrade service 464 to Quality Bus status, there would be a need to market this route as such a service but the southern end of the route was complicated as it consisted of three separate journey patterns that combined together to form a frequent service from Whitworth into Rochdale. In order to simplify this, from 18th July 2004, services 446 and 447 were extended from Shawclough to Wallbank to provide the means for

Wallbank passengers to reach Rochdale. This resulted in a Monday to Friday daytime service 464 which consisted of a 10 minute headway Accrington to Bacup and a 15 minute headway Bacup to Rochdale augmented from Shawforth to produce eight buses an hour into Rochdale. Over the next year, the Quality Bus contribution from Lancashire County Council saw all kerbs raised and new shelters built between Accrington and Bacup, so that service 464 was further revised from August 2005 to produce a more readily understandable timetable. All buses now ran throughout the route, at least every ten minutes Monday to Friday, every 15 minutes on Saturday and every 30 minutes on Sundays.

Greater Manchester PTE contract conditions require buses no older than 15 years and so, during the summer of 2004, the decision was made to replace the 'C' registered Olympians which had arrived in 1998 from London Central. Their replacements were eight newer 'S' registered Volvo Olympians, with single door bodies by Northern Counties, from another London operator, Metrobus, and this enabled the 'G' registered Olympians to be cascaded to Lancashire school bus duties.

As noted before, Optare had initially produced only a normal width Solo, but after protracted discussions they agreed to produce a narrow bodied version, marketed as 'Slimline' and Rossendale took the first examples of this vehicle type, fitted with an uprated version of the Cummins engine which had served so well in the Metroriders and Darts. Delivery of the first nine low floor vehicles took place in September 2004 and began to appear on Rochdale-based routes requiring smaller buses. Their success led to further orders and by March 2005, a total of 23 such vehicles had completely ousted all Metroriders, the Darts bought from Metroline in 1998 and 1999, and the first Darts bought new, numbered 101 to 105.

Contracted evening and Sunday services, operated on behalf of Greater Manchester PTE, were revised from 24th October 2004. This produced a new pattern of services between Bury and Rochdale comprising two hourly services, 468 (via Cutgate and Greave) and 469 (direct) which combined to produce a co-ordinated 30 minute service. Both services were operated by Rossendale Transport. The changes also meant the diversion of evening and Sunday service 433 to operate via the new leisure complex at Sandbrook Park.

A more momentous change from this date was the near total withdrawal of First Bus service 90

Optare Solo number 63 is shown operating the Bacup Circular service 21 in March 2007. *(HP)*

which operated every 30 minutes between Rawtenstall, Brandlesholme, Bury and Manchester. A few Monday to Friday peak journeys remained between Stubbins and Manchester, but generally Stubbins (and parts of Edenfield) no longer had an off-peak service to Bury. The result of this was that service 482 was diverted via the Woodlands Road area of Edenfield and service 484 (Accrington to Bury) was diverted to serve Stubbins. This milestone meant that First Bus no longer operated in the Borough of Rossendale except for a few peak hour Monday to Friday journeys.

The introduction of the CountyRider flexible bus service, in June 1995, had been confined to Tuesday and Friday operation but over the years, it had built up a regular clientele, so much so that bookings were being refused at certain times. The ROAR report (Rural Opportunities Across Rossendale), produced by the Countryside Commission in 2004, identified a number of communities within the Borough that were not served by any form of public transport and other instances where transport security issues and lack of knowledge were an obstacle to the use of many

facilities. The report urged Lancashire County Council and Rossendale Transport to build on the success of the CountyRider service and provide a Dial-A-Ride service throughout the week and particularly in the evening period.

Following lengthy periods of discussion, Lancashire County Council was able to obtain some external funding to purchase the four Mercedes Sprinter low floor buses from Rossendale Transport. Since 30th January 2005, one of these vehicles has been dedicated to the operation of services 2, 6 and 9 on Mondays to Saturdays whilst the other three are available to provide a Dial-A-Ride service between the hours of 07.00 and 23.00 Mondays to Fridays, 08.00 and 18.00 on Saturdays. Of the three vehicles, one is dedicated on Wednesdays and Saturdays to a semi-fixed flexible hourly service 21 linking Bacup

Number 84, H120 MOB, a Carlyle-bodied Dennis Dart was acquired from Metroline, London, in 1997 and is seen here in the centre of Rochdale in September of that year operating on the local service to Norden. *(RM)*

market with various areas in the east of the Borough.

The advantage to the County Council was that they could foresee the flexibility of the CountyRider being an alternative to the provision of rural and evening facilities provided by the more expensive mainstream bus services. An immediate effect of this was the withdrawal, from 30th January, of local routes 8 (Stonefold) and 15 (Cowpe) together with all service 244 journeys between Rawtenstall and Norden.

The CountyRider was one of the first services in the country to take advantage of new registration procedures which enabled the payment of BSOG (BUS SERVICES OPERATORS' GRANT *ie* fuel tax rebate) for all mileage operated. The service has been a huge success and, at the UK Bus Awards held in November 2006, CountyRider only just lost out as winner but was named as the highly commended runner-up for the Claudia Flanders Memorial Accessibility Award.

During the summer of 2005 Blazefield (Burnley & Pendle) drivers announced to passengers that the company was consulting about withdrawal of route 243 between Burnley, Rawtenstall and Bolton. These were the journeys that had been operated by Rossendale prior to 24th February 2003 when they had reluctantly had to relinquish them because of staffing problems and once confirmation was received of the date of the proposed change, Rossendale Transport immediately registered an hourly service 273 between Holcombe Brook and Bolton, the opportunity being taken to better inter-time the journeys with service 480 at the Bolton end of the route. Whilst Lancashire County Council was happy that service X43, now observing all stops, would adequately serve the needs of passengers between Burnley and Rawtenstall, they felt it necessary to subsidise an extension of service 273 through to Rawtenstall rather than terminating at Holcombe Brook. This resulted in a new interworking cycle, based on Rawtenstall, covering services 244 and 273 and Helmshore Circular services 11 and 12.

From 28th August, service 464 was completely simplified as described earlier, and in a similar simplification, the service 447 route variation via Bentley Street was withdrawn and all buses operated between Rochdale and Whitworth as service 446 journeys.

Despite increased staff recruitment, it was still not keeping pace with the exodus of staff, many of whom were now reaching retirement age. In order to address the problem and get the company back on track, it was agreed to recruit Polish drivers. Poland had recently joined the European Community and consequently there was a surfeit of trained bus drivers in Poland because of the need for Polish companies to become more commercially aware. Twelve such recruits joined the company early in October 2005 but needed training in language skills and different driving techniques and so they only started to become available for general driving duties from January 2006. Since then, most of these Polish staff have remained with the company and three Czech drivers have also been recruited – Rossendale is now truly a multi-national company.

From 3rd January 2006, in order to capture a large scholar flow between Burnley and the Bacup & Rawtenstall Grammar School (based in Waterfoot), arrangements were made to extend suitable service 483 morning and afternoon peak journeys to and from Burnley. At the same time, Lancashire County Council agreed to provide financial assistance to extend hourly off-peak and Saturday journeys on service 483 from Water to Burnley. In return, a further extension to Burnley General Hospital was provided commercially by Rossendale Transport. With good publicity and high quality low floor vehicles, this facility has been a great success, in complete contrast to when the service last operated in the year 2000. The extension to Burnley allowed the withdrawal of Saturday service 19, replaced by an hourly Saturday service on route 9 between Foxhill Drive and Rawtenstall.

On the same date, it was announced that the majority shareholding in Blazefield had been sold to Transdev, a French company, which had recently purchased other bus operations in the United Kingdom.

At the start of 2006, Lancashire County Council announced its intention to withdraw many contracted services throughout the county. As part of the consultation Rossendale Transport agreed changes to evening and Sunday services rather than face wholesale withdrawal. This resulted in the combination of the existing contracted journeys from Balladen to Rawtenstall (service 482), Rawtenstall to Edgeside (service 1) and

Rawtenstall to Water (service 483), which were replaced, from 23rd April 2006, by new hourly service 482 from Balladen to Water via Rawtenstall, Newchurch and Edgeside. On Sundays this service was combined with the commercial journeys on service 483 to form an hourly Bury to Water via Edgeside service. Together with an hourly Helmshore Circular service, journeys now cease after approximately 20.00 hours and passengers are advised to use the CountyRider service after these times.

After the arrival of the final Optare 'Slimline' Solos in March 2005, the only other acquisitions have been secondhand vehicles. In November 2005 three vehicles, only just over a year old, arrived following the demise of South Wales independent operator 2-Travel. These introduced both new chassis and body makes into the fleet, the vehicles being MAN 14.220 low floor single-decks with MCV Stirling bodywork.

Similar bodies, but built by MCV's predecessor, Marshall, appeared in June 2006 with the purchase of two Dart SLFs which had formerly been in the Widnes-based Halton Transport fleet. Despite being of low floor design, these buses did not have individual seats, ramps nor did they have a dedicated area for wheelchair and buggy users. Consequently, they were painted yellow and are used exclusively on peak hour school services.

Another four secondhand buses were acquired in August, these being Dart SPDs fitted with ALX 300 bodywork by Alexander. Despite having individual passenger seating these vehicles did not have ramps or an area for wheelchairs and buggies. Work was undertaken to address these shortcomings and upgrade them to EASYRIDE standards. After VOSA inspection (the former Vehicle Inspectorate inspection, and now the VEHICLE & OPERATOR SERVICES AGENCY inspection), they entered service on route 464 from October 2006.

Coachways Limited had been set up as a wholly owned subsidiary of Rossendale Transport, following the sale of Ellen Smith (Tours) Limited on 23rd May 2002. During the summer of 2006, a decision was made to wind down the Coachways operation and so, from September 2006, the school buses and regular local contracts previously operated by Coachways passed to Rossendale Transport. To operate these contracts, four coaches were transferred to Rossendale ownership with

effect from 1st September. These consisted of 300 (Dennis Javelin with 48 seat Plaxton Premiere 350 bodywork), 358, 359 (Volvo B10M with 48 seat Plaxton Expressliner bodywork) and 366 (Bova Futura with 53 seats).

From 1st April 2006, free fares were introduced for concessionary travellers within their own Borough area, but a further development was that GMPTE pass holders could now travel free beyond the boundary to Accrington. To cater for this demand, route 484 (Accrington to Bury) was increased to a regular two hourly service, Monday to Saturday, from 6th September 2006 and then further increased to hourly from 16th April 2007.

The year 2007 heralded a notable landmark in the history of municipal bus operation in the Rossendale area as this year marks 100 years since the first motorbuses were evaluated by the former Haslingden and Rawtenstall Corporations. To celebrate this, two of the 'S' registered Volvo Olympians have been repainted in the former liveries of Haslingden Corporation (fleet number 23) and Rawtenstall Corporation (fleet number 24). Both buses entered service in their new guise during March and April.

Following comments from passengers, service 464 was further improved from 16th April 2007 by reducing through journey times by the omission of Pennine Road Estate in Bacup. A new 'Pennine Road Shuttle' was introduced operating every 15 minutes between Pennine Road and Bacup where connections (and through fares) are available towards both Rochdale and Accrington. From the same date, services in the west of the Borough were improved with an increase in service 484 to produce an hourly service between Accrington, Haslingden and Bury.

Not content with celebrating its history and the achievements of a century of service, Rossendale Transport continues to look forward and is intent on maintaining its status as one of the few remaining municipally-owned passenger transport businesses in the country. In fact, it is now the last survivor of a long line of Lancashire Municipal bus undertakings that once served vast tracts of the Red Rose County. In recent times, neighbouring Blackburn has been sold to French-owned Transdev. Preston Bus is now wholly-owned by its employees and Blackpool, although still in public ownership, is now owned by Blackpool Unitary Authority and therefore not (to be politically correct) a true Lancashire operation.

The question may be asked, 'Why has Rossendale succeeded in maintaining a municipal transport undertaking in the deregulated age when many larger operators opted out and sold to private companies?' There has been determination from Rossendale Council to retain control combined with good management and an enthusiastic workforce which have worked together to provide the profitable company that exists today. In 1984 David Johnson, the leader of Rossendale Council, is quoted as saying, " The latest figures from the Transport Department are a disaster for any business, we must put our house in order and run an efficient service." The losses for the year ending 31st March 1985 were around £500,000.

How did it happen? Rossendale had to be reactive because of aggression from Greater Manchester Buses but in the end good sense prevailed and opportunities to expand into other areas were taken and the Company gained a reputation for reliability. The Company has been at the forefront of vehicle developments, being one of the first users of the Dennis Dart and purpose built minibuses as distinct from van-derived products. Low floor easy access vehicles were introduced at an early stage and the introduction of further vehicles of this type has, together with good presentation and publicity, resulted in growth of passenger numbers. These factors combined with slim management and administration structures have brought the company to its present situation.

Rossendale has much to celebrate in its centenary. As seen on the rear cover, in addition to having two buses painted in previous liveries, the event is to be celebrated with an Open Day based at Rawtenstall Depot on Saturday 28th July 2007.

Number 4, one of four Mercedes Benz Sprinter minibuses, with unusual German-built Koch body, was working local service 21 in Bacup when photographed in October 2005. *(MB)*

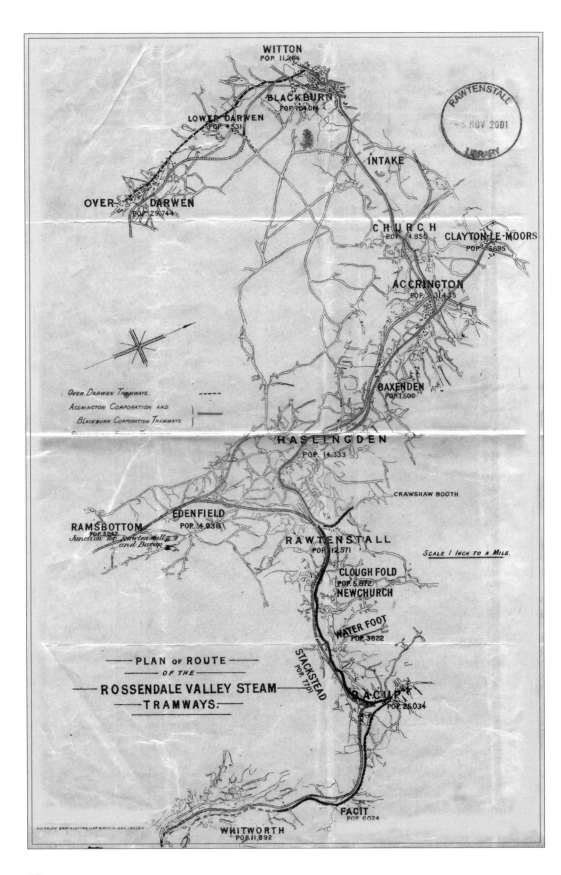

WITTON
POP. 11,364

BLACKBURN
POP. 104,014

LOWER DARWEN
POP. 4,531

INTAKE

OVER DARWEN
POP. 29,744

CHURCH
POP. 14,856

CLAYTON-LE-MOORS
POP. 8695

ACCRINGTON
POP. 31,435

BAXENDEN
POP. 1,500

Over Darwen Tramways.
Accrington Corporation and
Blackburn Corporation Tramways

HASLINGDEN
POP. 14,333

CRAWSHAW BOOTH

EDENFIELD
POP. 14,930

RAMSBOTTOM
POP. 5242
Junction for Rawtenstall
and Bacup.

RAWTENSTALL
POP. 12,971

SCALE 1 INCH TO A MILE.

CLOUGH FOLD
POP. 5,872

NEWCHURCH

WATER FOOT
POP. 3822

PLAN OF ROUTE
OF THE
ROSSENDALE VALLEY STEAM
TRAMWAYS.

STACKSTEAD
POP. 7701

BACUP
POP. 25,034

FACIT
POP. 6024

WHITWORTH
POP. 11,892

WATERLOW BROS & LAYTON, LIMD, BIRCHIN LANE, LONDON.

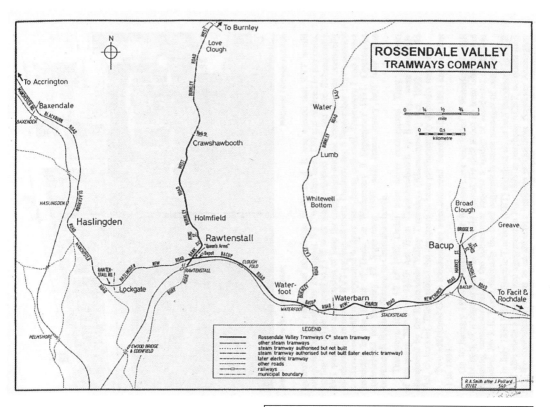

The origins of Public Transport in the Rossendale Valley owe much to the steam tramway which was originally seen as a means of connecting Rochdale, Bacup and Accrington through Rawtenstall and Haslingden as part of the Manchester, Bury, Rochdale and Oldham empire.

The mighty BET (British Electric Traction Co) decided to invest, hoping to acquire and electrify the system and add it to its own empire, but, as recorded elsewhere, local squabbling meant this never happened.

Haslingden became important as the connecting point, and its tracks saw steam and electric trams until 1932. The two maps, opposite and above, give the local topography, but note that the full page illustration opposite, a masterpiece of the map maker's art, has north at roughly ten-past on the clock face, and not at twelve o'clock as would be more normal. When the three undertakings were formed they operated over the same territory, with inter-working, and Accrington's steam and electric trams also appeared. For a fuller explanation *Great British Tramway Networks* by Bett and Gillham is recommended. *(RLIB)*

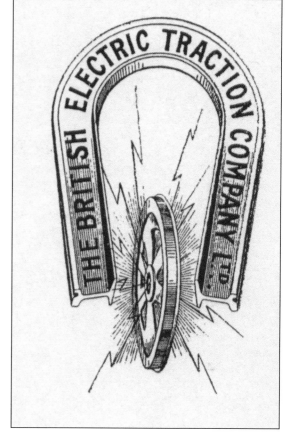

The famous Magnet-and-Wheel symbol of the BET Company, carried proudly on its trams, and, later, buses. *(STA)*

THOMAS GREEN & SON,
LIMITED,
Smithfield Iron Works, Leeds
AND
SURREY WORKS,
BLACKFRIARS ROAD, LONDON, S.E.

ENGINEERS AND MANUFACTURERS OF
GREEN'S IMPROVED LOCO-TYPE TRAMWAY ENGINES
With either Inside or Outside Cylinders,
HIGH PRESSURE OR COMPOUND PATTERN.
ALSO TANK LOCOMOTIVES & LIGHT RAILWAY ENGINES AND VAUX'S PATENT TRAMWAY COUPLINGS.

These Engines may be seen at work on the following Tramway Companies' Lines, viz :—

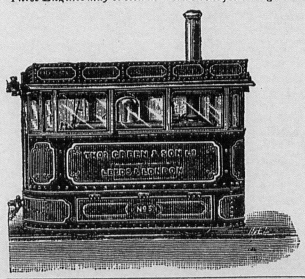

The Bradford & Shelf,
The Dundee & District,
The Bradford Tram and Omnibus,
The Blackburn and Over Darwen,
The Leeds,
The Accrington Corporation,
The Birmingham and Midland,
The Blackburn Corporation,
The Rossendale Valley,
The Drypool and Marfleet, Hull,
The Wolverton and Stony Stratford,
St. Helen's,
AND OTHERS.

PATENT LIFT FOR TRAMWAY ENGINES,
TOOLS AND FITTINGS FOR TRAM-ENGINE SHEDS.
OVERHEAD TRAVELLERS, HAND-POWER AND STEAM CRANES.
PATENT STEAM ROAD ROLLERS, TRACTION, STATIONARY, AND VERTICAL ENGINES AND BOILERS COMBINED.
STEAM WINCHES, PUMPS, &C.
Specifications, Price Lists, and References on Application.

The Steam Tram Era in Rossendale

Public street transport in most British towns began with horse trams, but the steep terrain in the Rossendale Valley area ruled this out. Steam trams were seen as one solution, and in 1886 the first such powered examples began operating in Accrington, with Rossendale following in 1888.

The steam tram was in effect a small railway locomotive, but, because of stringent legislation to satisfy owners of horses and horse drawn transport such as carts for the carriage of goods, these tram engines were required to consume their own steam – so as not frighten the aforesaid horses – and were also obliged to enclose their moving parts right down to ground level.

Steam was condensed, usually by tubes along the roof of the engine, and metal plating – skirts – hid the wheels and motion.

The trailers, usually double-decked, were enclosed, but with open staircases, as seen in the illustrations and also in the advertisement below.

Although several of the overseas tramway museums have working examples of tram engines and trailers, no such specimens have survived here. One good British example, at the National Tramway Museum, at Crich, in Derbyshire, consists of a static exhibit with a Beyer, Peacock-built engine and a typical (replica) trailer.

As the text explains the steam tram era in the Rossendale Valley lasted longer than anywhere else in the British Isles but, although the historical importance of the engines was recognised, in the depressed years of the late 1920s sadly no one was prepared – or able – to provide a home for the last survivor.

Facing page: A trade advertisement for Green's tramway engines, the make used in the Rossendale Valley. Note that Accrington and Rossendale are both listed as customers. *(STA/MTMS)*

Below: Milnes and Starbuck were among the pioneers of tramcar building. Note the capacity of the double-deck car, up to 100 passengers being capable of being accommodated. *(STA/PF)*

GEORGE F. MILNES & CO.,
(Successors to The Starbuck Car and Wagon Company, Limited)
TRAMWAY & LIGHT RAILWAY CARRIAGE WORKS,
Cleveland Street,
TELEGRAPHIC ADDRESS:
"TRAMVIA, BIRKENHEAD."
BIRKENHEAD.

BOGIE TRAMWAY CAR.
(With Upper and Lower Saloons enclosed.)
From 50 to 100 Passengers.

NARROW GAUGE RAILWAY CAR

Two of the Accrington Company's steam trams shown in Haslingden Town Centre, a view believed to have been taken in 1895 but everything is already looking down-at-heel. *(RLIB)*

A fine view of Rossendale Valley Tramways Steam tram No. 6 at Bacup. Note the application of advertisements, even on the front of the engine's steel panels. The reference to the 'armoured tram' reminds us that tanks and battleships were very much in people's minds at that time. *(RLIB)*

Above: On the last Monday of March 1908, Haslingden Corporation began work at Baxenden on the conversion of the tramways from steam to electrical operation. Here the Mayor, Alderman Hamilton, and the Chairman of the Tramways and Electricity Committee, Alderman Barlow, each take a crowbar to mark the occasion by lifting the first of the setts ready for the new track to be laid. *(RLIB)*

Below: The end of the road for the steam trams, together with their wooden trailers, shown below being broken up after withdrawal from service. In later years it would be quite common for such wooden bodies to find homes as sheds and chicken coops – some even became dwelling places or weekend holiday homes. As late as the end of the 20th Century such relics could still be found in fields or gardens, and some have been used as the basis of restoration projects. *(RLIB)*

A steam tram engine, with replica trailer, both similar the above, can be seen at the Crich Tramway Museum near Matlock. *(RLIB)*

This 40-seater Critchley-Norris double-deck open top bus, registered B 2064 and carrying the name *The Rossendale*, was purchased by the Rossendale Carriage Company of Bacup in 1906 and operated a service between Rawtenstall and Burnley. It is shown here proceeding in stately fashion up the centre of the road at Crawshawbooth, and again below posed for the photographer. The ladies would be considered adventurous in such a position, and a straw hat would require a very strong ribbon to keep it in place. *(RLIB)*

Ben Barnes and Son, Rawtenstall, were later taken over by Ellen Smith tours. Many years prior to this takeover they operated this Leyland RAF type charabanc named Lady Mary. There would appear to be a certain air of no-nonsense from the ladies on the outing – no bottles of beer stacked on the back seat this time perhaps! *(RLIB)*

A Daimler charabanc belonging to Ashworth Greenwood, on a men-only day out from Orama Cotton Mill, Whitworth in 1922. It was photographed just after setting off from the Hallfold Mill. Hats and caps would need to be held on tightly when the driver put his foot down, and there would need to be much brushing of clothes to get rid of the dust from the unmade roads when they got back home. *(RLIB)*

RAMSBOTTOM

Ramsbottom had one depot, at Stubbins Lane, where the transport offices were situated. Operation began in 1913 when Ramsbottom UDC became a trackless tramcar (trolleybus) operator, having accepted the fact that it could not afford the cost of building a tramway.

The maroon livery meant that its vehicles were often mistaken for neighbouring Rawtenstall's.

When amalgamation of those two undertakings was proposed, Ramsbottom made it clear it wanted no part, and remained alone. Local Government changes meant that it eventually became part of Greater Manchester and its transport undertaking was swallowed up by SELNEC.

MANAGERS	
J WILD	1913-1920
S PARSONS	1920-1951
LT MERRALL	1951-1967
J MORT	1967-1969

Ramsbottom's first trolleybus, No. 1, photographed on the first day of operation, 14th August 1913. The chassis was a Railless Electric Traction Co. production, the company name reflecting its product range, and the body was built for the RET company by Charles Roe, whose Cross Gates Carriage Works would soon become a respected name in the bus-building industry. *(RLIB)*

Facing page: Ramsbottom Trolleybus No. 4 with staff and horse drawn tower wagon for access to the overhead wires, posed at the depot. Another version of this photograph shows the name above the door as 'RAMSBOTTOM TRAMWAYS' despite the fact that the council did not operate trams – perhaps RAMSBOTTOM TRACKLESS TRAMWAYS seemed pretentious, or perhaps the stone mason did his work before the decision to create a trolleybus system was finally taken. *(RLIB)*

One of the second batch of Ramsbottom's trolleybuses, numbered 5 and 6, at Ramsbottom Station with driver Jack Holt. The bodies were by Lockwood and Clarkson and it was said that these were more comfortable than the original vehicles. *(RLIB)*

A fine view as one of the original vehicles heads up Bolton Road North, from Stubbins towards Edenfield. Ramsbottom's Manager, Sidney Parsons, later arranged for his son to be apprenticed to Charles Roe at the Leeds Cross Gates coachbuilding factory. *(RLIB)*

An unidentified member of the fleet waits at the Holcombe Brook terminus, which, as so very often, was outside a local hostelry. The rural nature of the system is obvious – whoever thought a tramway could have paid its way here? *(RLIB)*

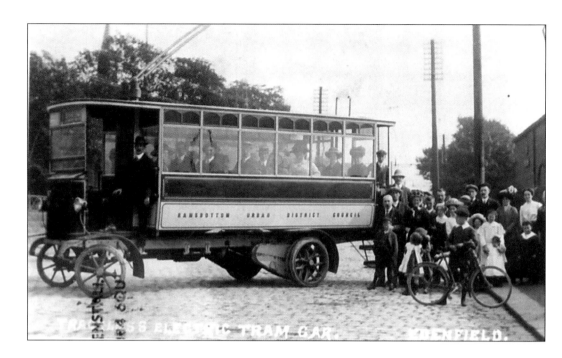

Great interest is shown as the photographer records this view at the junction of Blackburn Road and Market Street, Edenfield, near Edenfield school. Have the teachers brought the children out to see the event? *(RLIB)*

Number 7, below, had a chassis built by Thornycroft, to Railless design, and the body was built by Short Brothers. The vehicle was reinstated in 1925 after being out of service for some time, and on reinstatement, received the registration number TD 418. *(RMC)*

Number 5 was one of two vehicles supplied in 1915 which had bodies by Lockwood and Clarkson. When registration of trolleybuses became compulsory in 1921 it received the number TB 8573. The photographer has captured the turning circle in the overhead wires, but who were the gentlemen in the saloon with their straw boaters and bowler hat? *(RMC)*

Ramsbottom's first motor buses were Thornycrofts, built in Basingstoke in Hampshire, numbered 23/24/26 and supplied in 1922. This is No.10, one of five supplied two years later in 1924, and it has a body by Hall, Lewis of north London, later to become Park Royal Coachworks Ltd and later still Park Royal Vehicles Ltd. From the placing of this order we can take it that trolleybus number 7 must have been considered satisfactory. *(RMC)*

The first Leyland buses were purchased in 1927, and this is No.15, a PLSC1 model with Leyland body. This make of chassis, designed specifically for passenger work, as opposed to most up to that time which were adapted goods models, became a runaway success for the manufacturer and Ramsbottom stayed with Leyland for its buses until the end of UDC operation in 1969. *(RMC)*

This Leyland PLSC Lion, number 19, TE 6075, with Roe bodywork built in 1929, was photographed by Roe's photographer. It marked the beginning of the association between Leyland chassis and Roe bodywork which continued through to the post-war period. The thick black body lining marks the Roe trademark teak waistrail. *(STA/Roe)*

Following the success of its PLSC Lions, number 23, an example of the later LT5 model, entered the fleet. Once again carrying Leyland-built bodywork, it was photographed by the makers close to the factory when new and ready for collection by the UDC's driver. *(BCVM ref. 10730)*

Above, left and top facing: In 1934 two Leyland LT5A models, numbers 10 and 11, with bodies by Chas H Roe of Leeds were purchased. These were once again petrol-engined, four-cylinder, lightweight vehicles. The revised and much more purposeful front-end design is a distinct improvement over the previous model, as is the handsome bodywork, although the interior is rather forbidding. Number 11 is shown outside the Cross Gates works before the new office block was added, as seen opposite in the lower illustration. *(STA/Roe)*

Facing page, top: This Leyland LT5, No. 12, TJ 2639, was photographed by the railway cutting outside the Crossgates Carriage Works of Charles Roe before delivery in 1933. The later LT5A model incorporated a redesigned front end as seen on the lower photograph. *(STA/Roe)*

Posed in a place often used for photographs, outside the coachbuilder's offices in Leeds, is No. 6, a 1938 Roe-bodied Leyland Tiger TS8. The Tiger featured a six-cylinder engine and was Leyland's top of the range heavyweight single-decker. It was one of two supplied at this time and both remained in service until 1960. *(RMC)*

Roe bodies continued to be purchased after the war and No.19 was one of three Leyland PS1 (Post-war Single Tiger) models so fitted and supplied in 1947. It is shown here, in April 1954, in Bury with a Bury Corporation Northern Counties-bodied double-decker behind. Roe's distinctive teak waistrail can be discerned on both these single-deckers. *(RM)*

The first double-deckers to be purchased by Ramsbottom arrived in 1947 numbered 20-25 and were Leyland-bodied Leyland PD2/1 models. Number 22 is shown in Bury in April 1954, with another from the same batch behind, and also a Bury Corporation double-decker. *(RM)*

Ramsbottom purchased its first underfloor engined single-deckers in 1950 in the form of three Leyland Royal Tigers with Roe bodies numbered 26-28. The first of these, right, was photographed in Bury in April 1952 about to depart to Rawtenstall via Ramsbottom. *(RM)*

Two years later 1952 saw the arrival of another Leyland Royal Tiger, but this time with the characteristic body produced by Leyland for this chassis. It is loading in Bury for the journey to Rawtenstall in April 1954 with the destination blind still showing 'Bury via Ramsbottom'. *(RM)*

Below: A fine portrait by one of the Leyland photographers of Ramsbottom No. 30 before delivery to its new home. Cherished mark collectors will no doubt find the vehicle's registration number of interest. *(STA/LM)*

Only one bus was purchased in 1951, this being a Leyland PD2/1 again with Leyland body, numbered 29. It differed from the 1947 examples in having sliding rather than drop-down opening windows, and is shown at Ramsbottom in May 1966, still looking good despite by then being 15 years old. *(RM)*

Ramsbottom purchased no new vehicles between 1952 and 1961 when this Leyland PD2/24 with East Lancashire Coachbuilders body arrived and was numbered 1. This was the first time that Ramsbottom had purchased from ELCB. It is awaiting departure from Rawtenstall to Bury on 29th April 1967. On 1st November 1969 it became SELNEC No. 6401. Sadly the classic radiator has given way to the 'tin-front'. *(RM)*

Number 1 was followed in 1962 by number 2, a Leyland PD2/30 also with East Lancashire Coachbuilders body, but with what is usually described as the 'St Helens Style' enclosed radiator. It was the last rear-entrance bus to enter the Ramsbottom fleet. Note that in the pictures on these two pages reversed style registration numbers have made their appearance. *(RM)*

Number 3, a Leyland PD2/30 with East Lancashire body, arrived in 1963 and was Ramsbottom's first double-decker to have a front-entrance, a feature which was to be specified for all future double-deckers in the fleet. It was photographed at Holcombe Brook on a gloomy day in April 1963. *(RM)*

The 1965 addition to the Ramsbottom fleet was this ELCB-bodied Leyland PD3/1A, above, the first 30ft long double-decker to joint the undertaking. It was numbered 4 and differed from No. 3 in having a sliding rather than folding door. It is shown in Bury in September 1969, just over a month before the undertaking passed to SELNEC. *(RM)*

Ramsbottom's No. 12 was an Albion Aberdonian, with 31-seat Weymann body, purchased from Warrington Corporation in 1967 for the Holcombe Village service, and it is shown outside the depot. It had been new to Halifax Joint Omnibus Committee. *(RM)*

Number 11, a Leyland PD3/4 with ELCB bodywork, brought fame to Ramsbottom in that it was the last front-engined conventional double-decker to be delivered to an operator in Great Britain. Although ordered by Ramsbottom, and finished in its livery, it was actually delivered to SELNEC in November 1969. It is shown here in Bury on 30th March 1970. Happily, it survives in preservation, in immaculate condition. *(RM)*

HASLINGDEN

Haslingden had one depot, at John Street, and the transport offices were believed to also be situated in that building, although, as recorded in the text, the offices were actually authorised to be built first.

Motor bus operation began in 1907, and when the Rossendale Valley steam trams were withdrawn, and as recorded in the text, eight steam trams were purchased, together with seven trailers. These were withdrawn when electric trams began operating in 1908. Haslingden owned the track over which the later electric trams ran, but had no electric trams of its own. The undertaking ceased to exist as a separate entity after amalgamation in 1968.

Haslingden's first bus was this Leyland X model, with Leyland body dating from 1907, and registered B 2113. The body styling reflects that on early lorries produced by the company, formerly the Lancashire Steam Motor Company of Leyland. *(BCVM ref. 454)*

Haslingden withdrew its Leyland X model in 1908, and it was not until 1919 that a resumption of bus services was made with the purchase of this BSA 14 model with 12-seat body by Heap. It was replaced in 1920 by an Austin 2/3ton model. *(RMC)*

In 1924 Haslingden purchased this Guy B-type, with 26-seat body also by Guy Motors. Capacity was later reduced to 25 seats. It was numbered 1. Note the lifeguards under the high-slung bodywork. *(RMC)*

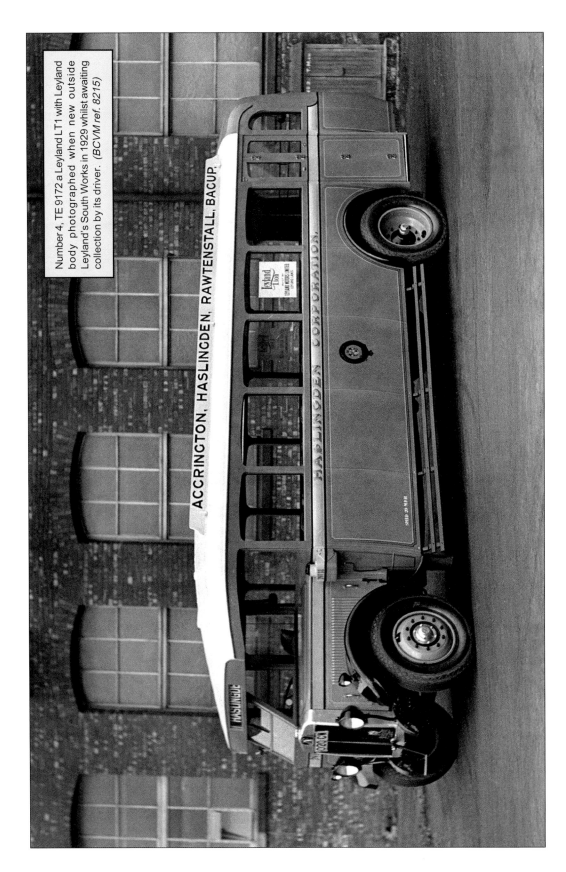

Number 4, TE 9172 a Leyland LT1 with Leyland body photographed when new outside Leyland's South Works in 1929 whilst awaiting collection by its driver. *(BCVM ref. 8215)*

In 1930 Haslingden purchased six new buses, the largest number ever purchased by them in one order. They were Leyland LT1 models with Leyland bodies numbered 5-10, and were required for tramway replacement. Number 6, complete with route board on the side for the Accrington to Bacup service, is shown heading for Rawtenstall. *(RMC)*

Haslingden's first double-decker was No.14, a magnificent-looking Leyland TD2 with Leyland highbridge body, which was photographed by the manufacturer when new. Note the gold lining on the blue and pale cream livery. *(BCVM ref. 10933)*

The year 1936 saw the arrival of two Leyland TD4 double-deckers with the recently introduced style of Leyland body, a design introduced following the appointment of Colin Bailey as Body Superintendent at South Works. Mr Bailey had previously been with MCW, and was recruited to solve problems with Leyland's previous model, the V-fronted body introduced on the TD3 Titan. The Bailey body, as this became known, was to remain with only detail changes up to the end of Leyland body production in 1953. It was considered a classic amongst double-deckers, with its unbroken gentle curved outline from roof to front offside wing. The Haslingden examples were numbered 18 and 19 and the latter was photographed by Leyland when new. *(LM)*

The Leyland metal-framed body had a good reputation, as had the chassis, and No.19 was still giving good service when photographed 15 years later *en route* to Bacup in Rawtenstall in June 1951, with a postwar Leyland PD2 with ELCB body from the Rawtenstall fleet standing behind *en route* to Burnley. *(LM)*

Number 20, a Leyland TD5 dating from 1937, and once again with Leyland body, was photographed in Haslingden in April 1954 when 17 years old. Thom's Castile soap and 'Say CWS and Save' were advertisements carried by buses in fleets throughout the land. *(RM)*

After Leyland Motors output was switched over to building tanks for the war effort, Haslingden was allocated three wartime double-deckers, this one being a Daimler CWA6. It is seen fitted with Brush bodywork to Ministry of War Transport relaxed utility specification, and was delivered in 1945. It was withdrawn in 1955. *(RM)*

Haslingden No. 25, GTD 497, was the operator's first postwar bus and was a Leyland PD1 with body built by Alexander of Falkirk to Leyland design. The photograph was taken at Leyland by one of Leyland's photographers, and the bus is clearly in grey. Was the final painting done at Leyland? *(LM)*

Number 26 was the second postwar double-decker and was a Leyland PD1A with Leyland body. It is shown in Haslingden in 1959. The bodywork on PD1 models continued right down to the lower mudguard edge, where the horn can be seen. The PD2 models which followed featured a cut back panel as seen below. *(RM)*

Leyland-bodied Leyland double-deckers continued to be the Haslingden standard in the immediate postwar period and No. 27, a PD2/1 model, joined the fleet in 1948. Rawtenstall's Queens Square Bus Station provides the setting for this view of No. 27 operating on the service from Accrington to Bacup in June 1951. *(RM)*

This page: two views of the final design of Leyland body supplied to Haslingden in 1953, just before the cessation of body building at Leyland. Number 11 was one of three numbered 9-11 on PD2/12 chassis. The upper photograph taken in March 1956 shows it passing through Rawtenstall *en route* from Bacup to Accrington. The lower photograph shows it in Accrington awaiting departure to Bacup in September 1963.

Facing page: Following the dramatic cessation of body building at Leyland, Haslingden turned to East Lancashire Coachbuilders for bodywork. With the recommencement of the numbering system at 1 there had been no new No. 5 because the original No. 5 supplied in 1930 was not withdrawn until 1951. This was rectified in 1954 with the arrival of this Leyland PD2/12 with ELCB body. It was still looking very smart when photographed near Rossendale Hospital twelve years later in March 1966. *(RM both)*

Another fine view of Leyland PD2 No. 5, advertising the local newspaper *The Haslingden Observer*, one of the many sources of information which the author has studied in the local libraries. *(RM)*

Driver and conductor relax and chat as they await departure from Bacup to Accrington with Haslingden No. 12, an East Lancashire-bodied PD2 dating from 1955. The driver will miss his mudguards when Atlanteans arrive! A Rawtenstall PD2, also ELCB-bodied, also waits behind. *(RM)*

This Roe bodied Leyland Royal Tiger PSU1/13, with its distinctive and impressive leaping Tiger badge, was new to Ramsbottom in 1950 but then acquired by Haslingden in 1962. It was numbered 15, and is shown in Haslingden in August 1963. Roe's distinctive trade-mark waistrail has been retained in the design. *(RM)*

Number 17, a Leyland Leopard L1 with East Lancashire body, was new in 1964 and was photographed in Haslingden when quite new in October 1964. The Tiger badge has been replaced by a Leopard on the front – there had been a lighter weight Tiger Cub between the two models. *(RM)*

The last vehicle supplied to Haslingden prior to the merger with Rawtenstall was No. 2, a Leyland PD3/14 with classic East Lancashire body depicting what many would consider to be British bus-building at its best. It is shown *en route* to Bacup in March 1968. *(RM)*

Still working from Accrington to Bacup, Haslingden No. 2 is seen again against a backdrop familiar at the time but much less common now, the gasholder for storing the town's gas. Alongside the bus, parked outside the dry cleaners, is one of Ford's new range of cars. *(DP)*

RAWTENSTALL

Rawtenstall transport offices were situated on the north side of Bacup Road, with the tram depot behind.

Operation began in 1907 with the first buses. Later when the Rossendale Valley steam trams were withdrawn in July 1909, as recorded in the text, two steam trams were purchased, to be used as snow ploughs.

Electric trams operated from October 1908 until March 1932, with a ceremonial closure one week later on 7th April, and the steam trams were withdrawn at the same time. Subsequently, in 1933, a replacement bus depot was built on the south side of the road, and is still in use today.

MANAGERS	
JK NORTH	1908-1909
CLE STEWART	1909-1930
F LYTHGOE	1931-1934
JE ORD	1934-1940
WH BARKER	1940-1945
LT MERRALL	1945-1969

Two views showing FA 159, the Rawtenstall Corporation Ryknield double-decker, on 23rd July 1908 following its crash at the junction of Cog Lane and Coal Clough Lane after being used by members of Bury and District Water Board to visit reservoirs. *(RMC; RLIB)*

The official opening of the Rawtenstall Corporation electric tramways on 15th May 1909. This view shows a decorated tramcar in Bacup Road, connecting with a bus to Burnley on Bank Street. Note the early motor car on the left. *(RLIB)*

Rawtenstall tram No. 3 on the Bacup route c1910. Built by the United Electric Car Co of Preston (UEC) the body is mounted on a 4-wheel Brill truck. The open balcony ends to the top deck are by now fairly standard in the tramway world – had Rawtenstall had trams earlier they would have been open-topped. *(RLIB)*

Facing page: Rawtenstall Corporation tram No. 14, one of the first 16 such cars, posed on Bacup Road with Mr Frank Lythgoe, the General Manager. The driver's platforms have now been vestibuled in the Corporation's workshop, but the balconies remain open. Note the long bamboo pole carried on the truck and used for turning the trolley round. *(RLIB)*

Following the first 16 balcony cars, two enclosed 4-wheelers were received from the Brush Company, numbers 17 and 18, in 1912, as seen above. Six single-deckers came next, numbered 19-24 for the Water route, and finally eight Brush bogie cars were delivered in 1921, as seen below. They had relatively short lives, the system closing in 1932. *(RLIB)*

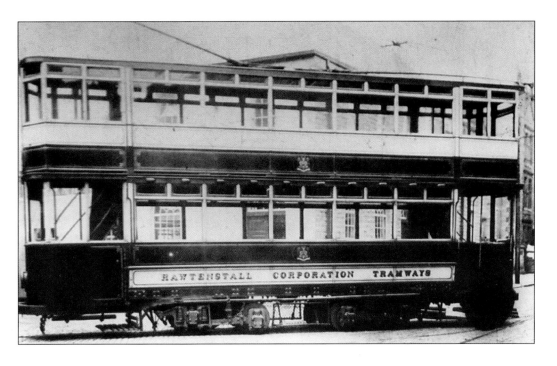

The last Accrington trams leave Haslingden for home in 1932. Some sources give the date as 30th April, but the Rawtenstall system closed on the 30th March, and the route was jointly worked. The headlamp location, in the upper dash panel rather than the normal lower position, was a feature of these cars. Accrington operated electric trams from August 1907 until January 1932, having 38 cars, of which 25 were double-decked. The Accrington, Blackburn, Darwen and Rawtenstall systems formed quite an extensive 4ft gauge network of which Haslingden's tracks were an integral part. *(RLIB)*

Accrington also had a fleet of 13 single-deck cars, as seen here, and used on the Church route. After the system closed five dating from 1915 (Nos. 28-30) and 1920 (Nos. 31/2) were sold to the Llandudno & Colwyn Bay Electric Railway, which regauged them and then operated them on its 3ft 6in gauge system until it closed in March 1956. *(RMC)*

The entrance to the old four track Rawtenstall tram depot with a selection of trams and bus No, 55, a 1931 Leyland TD1 with Leyland highbridge bodywork. *(RLIB)*

Farewell for trams as Frank Lythgoe, Walter Harker, H Walton and Frank Crankshaw pose with the decorated last tram, an enclosed bogie car, in March 1932. *(RLIB)*

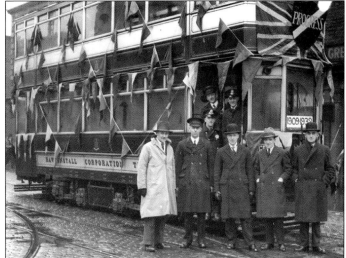

The photographers duly recorded all the events for posterity – the last trams and the replacing buses.

The cold, wet, March weather did not stop members of the local populace turning out to pay their respects to the old electric trams, and their famous steam snowplough forebear. *(RLIB)*

Single-deck No. 23 from the batch 19-24 survived as a shed for many years until purchased as a restoration project. Sadly, although it still exists, the necessary resources in terms of manpower and finance have not been available to allow the project to be completed. It had been hoped that the rebuilt car, on a replacement standard gauge truck, might one day operate in Manchester's Heaton Park with other restored electric trams. *(RLIB)*

Below: A fascinating interior view of the workshop, with its selection of bespoke tools, inside the tram shed. *(RLIB)*

Opposite: An even more fascinating interior view of the inside of the tram shed, with the replacement buses in full view. Left to right are TC 9004, one of the four Leyland SG9s of 1924; TD 8678 and TD 8679, the pair of 1927 PLSC1 Lions again with Leyland bodywork but showing differing liveries, and, almost hidden in the background, FA 157, the survivor of the two 1907-built Ryknield open toppers, taken out of service in 1910 but still in use as a tower wagon. *(RLIB)*

101

Above: Rawtenstall's long association with Leyland Motors began in 1924 with the delivery of the first buses since the ill-fated Ryknields. Six SG9s came, numbered 33-8, with dual-doorway Leyland bodies as shown above. The floor level was very high, as can be seen, and the steps must have been awkward to negotiate. The chassis design was innovative in that the driver was now located alongside the engine in a separate cab. (RMC)

Below: Rawtenstall then purchased two Leyland SG11 single-deckers in 1925, and numbered them 41/2. The first of the pair is shown here before delivery and the rear step arrangement again gives the clue as to the high floor. A second door can be discerned, in the narrow second bay, but the folding steps suggest that it is not the normal method of access, unlike the previous batch. (BCVM ref. 3319)

Facing page: The Leyland Lion PLSC type, produced in two lengths, became a success-story single-decker of the late 'twenties with examples in many fleets. Rawtenstall purchased four of the shorter model PLSC1 in 1927, and one of these, No. 43, was photographed by Leyland's photographer when new. (BCVM ref. 4100)

Leyland's new single-decker range was introduced to succeed the PLSC Lion model, and examples of the six-cylinder Tiger model entered the fleet first, in 1930, when numbers 47/8 were delivered. The body styling can be seen to have developed considerably since the SG9s of 1924. A four-cylinder model, the LT1 Lion was also introduced, and Rawtenstall purchased numbers 49-52 in that same year. *(BCVM ref. 7618)*

Leyland were always keen to show batches of vehicles in their publicity material, and when five single-deckers were added to the Rawtenstall fleet in 1931, in addition to the five recently delivered double-deckers, all five saloons were duly lined up for the camera. All were of Leyland manufacture, two being TS1 models and the other three being LT3 models, all with Leyland bodywork. In this view the Tigers are first and third from the left, numbers 58 and 59, whilst the Lions were numbered 60-62. *(BCVM ref. 10472)*

Rawtenstall TF 1099 fleet No. 47 a Leyland TS2 with Leyland body dating from 1930 passes the Melias store, a well-known name in the grocery trade in those days, as it operates on the already long-established joint service from Accrington to Bacup. *(CMC)*

Right: Number 60, from the 1931 batch of Leyland LT3 Lions, climbs one of the many hills out of the Rossendale Valley, this being a steady 1in7 prohibited to double-deckers. *(RMC)*

The arrival of the Leyland TD1 Titans, numbered 53-56, coincided with a change in the livery. The official Leyland photograph, left, shows the original lettering style between decks on No. 53, whilst the picture of No. 56 on the facing page clearly shows the change to the very neat style which lasted until the end of the undertaking's existence. *(STA/LM)*

After the demise of the trams the opportunity was taken to restart numbering the fleet at 1, and the Leyland Titans shown left and below were respectively numbers 1 and 13. Note the sign above the policeman's head pointing to a public telephone, and his white sleeves denoting that he was on point duty, directing traffic. Not that there was much! *(RMC)*

A view of the entrance to the new bus depot at the Bacup end showing the gantries for vehicle washing. Also visible is the name over the door – Rawtenstall Corporation Motors – still to be seen in 2007. *(RT)*

An internal view taken in April 1933 just before the official opening of the new bus depot built on the opposite side of Bacup Road to the tram depot. *(RT)*

Rawtenstall received two Leyland TD4 models numbered 21 and 22 with the latest V-front style of Leyland metal-frame body as illustrated here by No. 21 when new. This body design was, quite literally, a disaster and Leyland was obliged to rebuild many examples under warranty. These two must have been only marginally better than average, for both were earmarked to be rebodied as soon as wartime conditions allowed. *(LM)*

Even vehicles which had been trouble-free when new were usually suffering from neglect by 1945 and many operators found themselves with serviceable chassis carrying bodies which were beyond economic repair and, accordingly, embarked on rebodying programmes. The centre photograph shows No.18, a 1933 Leyland TD3, which with sister vehicle No. 17 was rebodied by Northern Coachbuilders of Newcastle upon Tyne in 1944 and 1945, the bodies being to the Wartime 'Utility' specification. Two Leyland TD4 models, Nos. 21 and 22 dating from 1935, were rebodied by HV Burlingham of Blackpool in 1946 and 1947. The lower photograph shows No. 22 in June 1948. The body design still shows traces of wartime specification in that window pans were not fitted. *(RM)*

Number 46, a Leyland TS8c, with Leyland body was one of two similar buses supplied in 1938 and was still giving service when photographed above in Rawtenstall in April 1954. A similar vehicle supplied in 1939 and numbered 50 has been preserved and regularly appears at rallies, as seen below. The deep header tank for the Autovac on the bulkhead confirms that the vehicle still has its torque-convertor, but the preserved example lost its unit in exchange for a conventional gearbox some time before withdrawal. *(RM upper, JAS lower)*

Postwar additions to the fleet commenced in 1947 and included Nos. 41-49, HTF 361-369, Leyland PD2/1 models with Leyland bodies, a type which was to figure prominently in the next few years. Number 47 is shown in Haslingden, operating on the Accrington to Bacup service, in June 1951. *(RM)*

In the restrictive wartime years Rawtenstall received only one complete new vehicle. It was a Guy Arab II, and when new carried a utility body by Massey Brothers of Wigan. In 1951 it received a new body by East Lancashire Coachbuilders, as seen here, and remained in service until 1964 despite being the only Guy in the fleet. It is shown in Rawtenstall in August 1953. *(RM)*

The following year, 1948, saw the arrival of another five Leyland PD2/1 for the Rawtenstall fleet, numbered 11-15, all with bodywork from East Lancashire Coachbuilders. *(RM)*

A further ten Leyland PD2/1 Titans arrived in 1949, this time all with Leyland bodies, and numbered 1-10. The seventh of the batch was photographed in Burnley. *(RC)*

Above: The first postwar intake of single-deckers for Rawtenstall arrived in 1949 and were two ELCB-bodied Leyland PS1 Tigers, Nos. 53/54, the first of which is shown in Rawtenstall in August 1953. *(RM)*

Two more single-deckers arrived in 1950 and were Leyland PS2/1 models, again with East Lancashire Coachbuilders bodies. One of these, No 56, was rebuilt to front entrance in 1962 for one-person-operation and is shown in this form in July 1962. *(RM)*

The last Leyland-bodied vehicles arrived in 1953, after which the company ceased manufacture of bus bodywork. Number 18 pictured above *en route* to Bacup in October 1964 illustrates the final style of Leyland double-deck bodywork, with window pans radiused at both top and bottom. The lower photograph shows sister vehicle No. 19 in April 1954 in an experimental livery incorporating only one cream band. Happily, this simpler livery was not adopted! *(RM)*

Following the cessation of bus bodybuilding at Leyland Motors, East Lancashire Coachbuilders became the regular supplier of both single- and double-deck bodies. Number 20, shown here in April 1954, was numerically the first of four supplied in 1953. *(RM)*

VTJ 734, shown in Rawtenstall Bus Station in April 1967, was numbered 63 when new in 1955 but was renumbered 27 in January 1961. It has an East Lancashire Coachbuilders body incorporating an enclosed radiator in the standard Leyland style of that time, often referred to as the 'tin front'. *(RM)*

This view in Rawtenstall in March 1956 shows Leyland Tiger Cub PSUC1/1 No. 57 with Weymann body, which arrived in the fleet in 1955. It was new in 1953 and had been a Leyland demonstrator on a chassis registered OTD 301. The body was transferred to this chassis when the original was scrapped. *(RM)*

Below: The only new vehicle in 1958 was this Tiger Cub PSUC1/5 with East Lancashire body, numbered 58, and shown in Rawtenstall Bus Station in March 1958. *(RM)*

Facing page: The 1964 delivery of double-deckers, the first since 1955, marked a return to the exposed radiator, the increase in length to 30ft, and the adoption of front entrance. The order comprised four Leyland PD3/4 with ELCB bodies numbered 30-33. The photograph, taken in Accrington in October 1964, shows the impressive length of these vehicles. *(RM)*

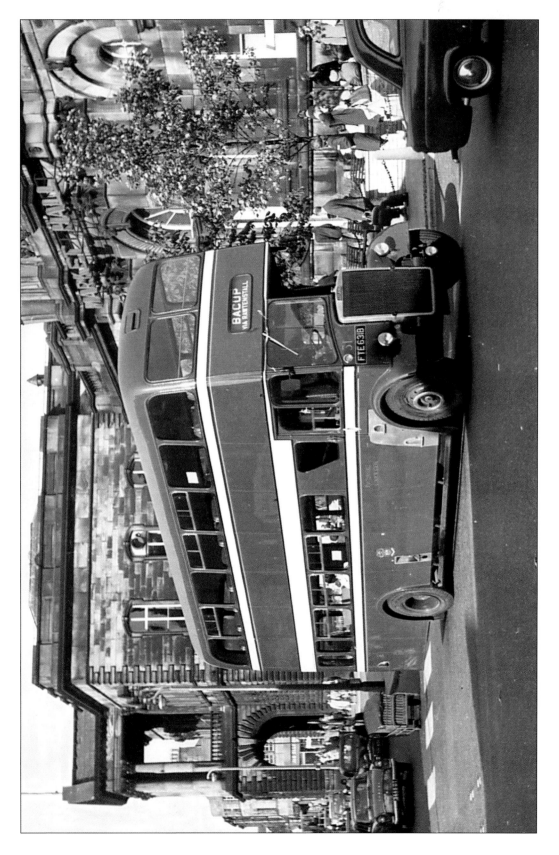

ROSSENDALE JOINT TRANSPORT COMMITTEE 1968-1974

ROSSENDALE BOROUGH TRANSPORT 1974-1986

The Joint Transport Committee was formed in 1968 and in 1974, following local Government reorganisation, became Rossendale Borough Transport, with all the vehicles operating from the Rawtenstall premises.

Approaching Burnley Bus Station in May 1971 is XTJ 939D, one of three double-deckers forming the last purchase by Rawtenstall Corporation before the formation of the Joint Committee. It carries fleet No. 39, the number allocated by Rawtenstall when it was new. *(RM)*

FTF 732B, a Leyland Leopard with its East Lancashire Coachbuilders body, new to Haslingden in 1964 as its No. 17, is seen in the town in December 1968 with 'Joint Transport Committee' fleetname and carrying fleet No. 48. *(RM)*

Number 36, a 1965 East Lancs-bodied Leyland PD3 new to Rawtenstall, passes through Edenfield in April 1970 *en route* from Bury to Water pursued by a learner in a Wolseley Hornet. *(BD)*

Passing through Rawtenstall on the trunk service from Bacup to Accrington in August 1970 is another East Lancs-bodied PD3, No. 41, which had been new to Rawtenstall in 1967. *(BD)*

The driver seems to be viewing the photographer with some suspicion as he leaves Rawtenstall Bus Station for Hall Carr in August 1970. The bus is No. 49, a Leyland Leopard carrying an East Lancs body, new to Haslingden Corporation as its No.18 in 1965. *(BD)*

East Lancs bodied-Leyland Leopard No. 60 arrives at Burnley Bus Station in October 1971 with the 13.15 departure from Rawtenstall. The service had only been converted to one-person-operation the previous Sunday. *(BD)*

Former Rawtenstall No. 6, a 1949 Leyland PD2 with Leyland body is shown in Bury awaiting departure to Edenfield in May 1971. On the earlier PD1 model the dash panel covered the offside front wing. *(BD)*

One of the last Leyland-bodied Leyland PD2s to be received prior to the cessation of bus body building at Leyland was No. 17, new to Rawtenstall in 1953. It is shown heading through Haslingden towards Bacup in March 1971 when 18 years old. The classic lines of this final version of Leyland double-deck body design are evident. *(BD)*

Looking very smart, despite being 18 years old, is No. 23, photographed at the Bacup terminus of the service from Accrington in February 1971. An East Lancs-bodied Leyland PD2, it was new to Rawtenstall in 1953. *(BD)*

Number 43, a Leyland PD2 with East Lancs body, travels through Haslingden *en route* from Bacup to Accrington in May 1972. It was new to Haslingden in 1957 as No.13, and was the first bus in the fleet to carry that number. It is now preserved. *(BD)*

Facing page: XTF 98D, an East Lancashire Coachbuilders-bodied Leyland PD3, was new to Haslingden in 1966 as its No.1. It is shown returning to Rawtenstall through Crawshawbooth in July 1974 as Rawtenstall Borough Transport No. 45, a number which it received on the formation of the Joint Committee. It would not have operated on this route in its Haslingden days. *(RM)*

East Lancs-bodied Leyland PD3 DTJ 960E was the last double-decker to be purchased by Haslingden Corporation. It was delivered in 1967 and carried fleet No. 2. When transferred to Rossendale Joint Transport Committee in 1968 it received fleet No. 46. It is shown arriving in Burnley in April 1975 when it operated as a duplicate to the 14.15 departure from Rawtenstall on service 291. In its Haslingden days it would not have operated to Burnley. *(BD)*

On 14th February 1976 East Lancs-bodied Leyland Leopard No. 66 departs Rawtenstall for Accrington with the Library and Parish Church in the background. It is being followed by a Ribble Leyland Atlantean with coach-seated MCW body, RRN 432, working on service X43 to Manchester. When originally delivered these vehicles, intended for medium distance express services, carried a cream livery with single red band. They were later painted in the drab NBC poppy Red livery used for normal service buses. *(BD)*

Leaving Rawtenstall for Accrington on 14 February 1976 is FTE 632B an East Lancs bodied Leyland PD3 new to Rawtenstall as No. 30 in 1964. It retained the No. 30 on the formation of Rossendale Joint Transport Committee. *(BD)*

On 3rd July 1976, East Lancs-bodied Leyland PD3 No. 35 was photographed passing the Yelloway Coach Station on Bloomfield Road, Blackpool. It had been hired to Hyndburn Transport who, in turn, had hired it to Ribble who used it to duplicate the 12.45 service No. 282 from Burnley to Blackpool. Despite being on hire to Hyndburn, the lower window sticker states it is on hire to Accrington Corporation ! Above this is another sticker, visible on the original photograph, reading 'on Hire to Ribble'. *(BD)*

Bristol RE number 7, YTC 307N, had received the new reversed livery when this photograph was taken in Rawtenstall in August 1983. It carries bodywork by East Lancashire Coachbuilders. *(RM)*

Number 52, a smaller Bristol LHS example, with Eastern Coach Works body, was purchased from London Country Bus Services in 1983, where the model was considered inadequate for the rigours of the Capital. It had been new in 1977 and is shown here in March 1984. *(RM)*

ROSSENDALE TRANSPORT LTD

The Limited Company was formed in 1986, in preparation for Deregulation, and for the first time the General Manager became Managing Director. The fleet continued to operate from Rawtenstall.

This Alexander Y-type- bodied Leyland Leopard was one of four similar vehicles dating from 1978 and bought from Kelvin Scottish in 1988. It was at Balladen in February 1988, shortly after purchase. *(RM)*

Seen below passing through Rawtenstall *en route* to Bury in May 1987, just shortly after delivery, is Leyland Olympian No. 88 with coach seated East Lancashire Coachbuilders bodywork. From a mechanical point of view it was apparently not a good vehicle, suffering regularly from engine overheating problems. *(RM)*

Leyland Atlantean number 27, which dated from 1982, was rebuilt with coach seating and is shown in appropriate coach livery at the Bacup Road stop in Rawtenstall *en route* to Bacup in April 1988. The large lettering on the upper-deck panels was eye-catching. Note the emergency exit towards the rear of the lower deck. *(RM)*

Seen at Bacup dropping down towards Rochdale on service 464 from Accrington in June 1988 is Atlantean No. 34 which had been purchased from Hyndburn Transport in 1987. The light accentuates the distinctive peak of the ELCB body design. *(RM)*

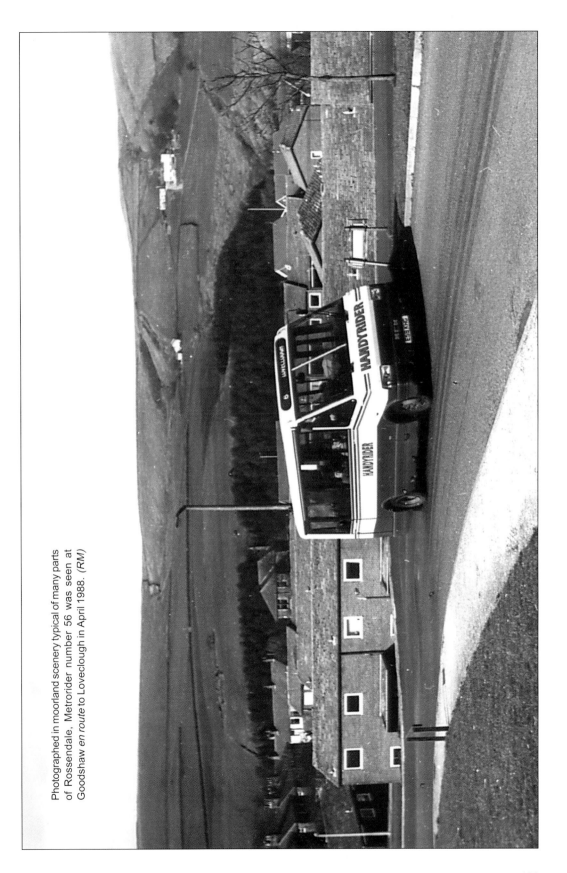

Photographed in moorland scenery typical of many parts of Rossendale, Metrorider number 56 was seen at Goodshaw *en route* to Loveclough in April 1988. *(RM)*

When photographed in Bacup on 7th June 1988, Bristol RE No. 12 was displaying the latest livery and had also been provided with a service number indicator to the offside of the destination display. Presumably located there for ease of changing by the driver, it would have been much more visible to passengers if it was on the nearside. *(RM)*

The destination display is again a key feature in this view, for it immediately confirms the original ownership of the vehicle. Photographed at Shawforth whilst travelling to Accrington in June 1988 is No. 45, one of seven Daimler Fleetlines with distinctive Northern Counties bodywork purchased from GM Buses in 1987. *(RM)*

Number 72, JDK 925P, a Leyland Leopard with Plaxton body dating from 1975 was purchased from GM Buses in 1987 and was photographed at Hall Carr in June 1988. New to Lancashire United and acquired by GM after LUT passed to that organisation following Local Government reorganisation in 1976, it was one of hundreds of buses sold by GM Buses following Deregulation in 1986. *(RM)*

Atlantean No. 19 carefully negotiates the street furniture as it leaves Bury for Rawtenstall on service 483 in May 1990. The small dark panel adjacent to the doorway on the front pillar is normally designed to be illuminated when the vehicle is used in driver-only operation. *(RM)*

This Leyland Tiger, No. 94 with East Lancashire body, was one of four bought new in 1989, the last new Leyland vehicles to be bought by Rossendale. It is shown at Middleton in April 1989. *(RM)*

Illustrating the variety of vehicle and operation by Rossendale is ECW bodied Leyland Leopard coach No. 176 acquired from Ambassador Travel (Anglia) Ltd . It was still carrying National Express livery, albeit with 'Rossendale' name above the front wheel arch when arriving at Preston Bus Station in May 1991. It was operating for Red Rose PTS on Leisurelink Service 72 from Blackpool to Seatoller in the Borrowdale Valley. *(BD)*

'All Change' read the rather appropriate advert on the side of Rossendale No. 46 when it was photographed in Manchester Piccadilly on 7th September 1991. It was operating on service 17 to Rochdale, a service which in years gone by had been the domain of Manchester and Rochdale Corporations as far back as tramcar days. It is ironic that the vehicle is an ex-GM Buses Leyland Atlantean with NCME body. *(BD)*

Heading out of Bury at the end of April 1993, and making for Manchester Piccadilly on service X76, is No. 77, UGG 369R, a Leyland Leopard which was new in 1977 but had just received this new bus body by East Lancashire Coachbuilders. The futuristic building behind the bus is part of the new Bury Interchange built by the Passenger Transport Executive. *(RM)*

Metrorider No. 63, one of the original batch of eight bought new in 1989, is shown against the background of Rawtenstall Parish Church on 7th May 1993. *(RM)*

B102 PHG a Leyland Olympian with East Lancashire Coachbuilders body was one of two purchased from Stevensons in 1993. It is shown in Valley Link livery leaving Rawtenstall for Manchester Piccadilly in May 1994. *(RM)*

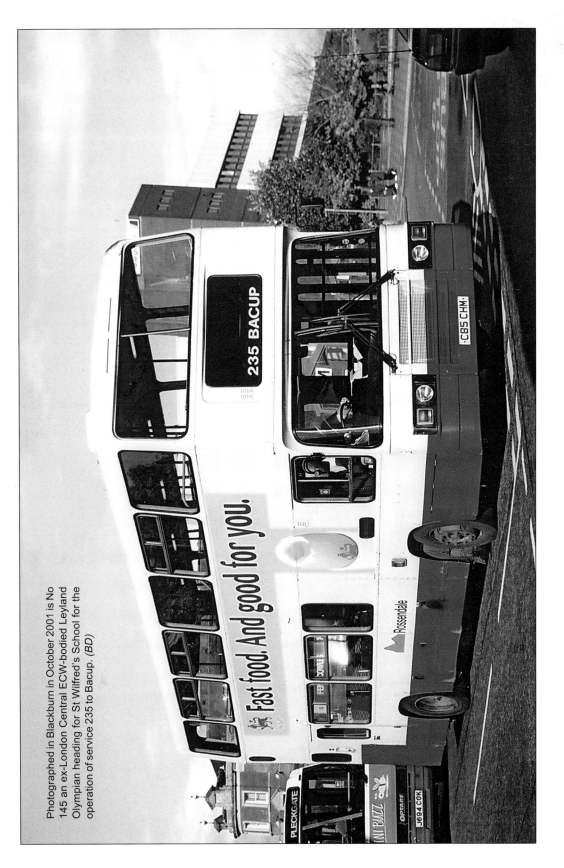

Photographed in Blackburn in October 2001 is No 145 an ex-London Central ECW-bodied Leyland Olympian heading for St Wilfred's School for the operation of service 235 to Bacup. *(BD)*

235 BACUP

Fast food. And good for you.

Rossendale

·C85 CHM·

PLECKGATE

MINI BUZZ

J694 COK

OPTARE

135

NOTES ON LIVERIES

Livery notes – Rawtenstall, Haslingden & Rossendale only

The earliest livery applications for the Haslingden and Rawtenstall fleets were blue. Haslingden 1 (TC 8581) was dark blue and white but from 3 (TE 5736) onwards, a light blue scheme was employed with some white relief and this later evolved into the light blue and cream of later years (Masons Blue).

Rawtenstall's Ryknield's were blue and cream, but perhaps the notoriety that beset this experimental pair of buses influenced the decision to paint all subsequent additions in maroon and cream and this was perpetuated throughout the life of the undertaking, although by the 1960s the shade was better described as a 'paeony' red.

The formation of the Joint Transport Committee saw future repaints and new deliveries emerge in a slightly lighter crimson lake colour, retaining various proportions of cream relief. In 1975, two of the new Bristol REs were painted in a reversed livery of mainly cream with crimson lake skirts and window sections, to denote their status as the front line Private Hire vehicles. This presaged further livery experiments that saw this scheme applied to the single-deck fleet from 1982. Prior to this, the arrival of the Atlanteans introduced more cream to the double-deck livery and this was also modified after a few years. The first all-over advertising bus made its debut in 1982, also on an Atlantean, with several others following over the next decade. The Leopard coaches of 1985 largely retained their former livery of white and red, with some minor detail changes, but this was later revamped into a much more prominent Rossendale Coach Hire brand after deregulation.

In October 1987, the last of the ex-Greater Manchester Fleetlines to be prepared for service was painted in a revised livery with the crimson lake skirt replaced by middle red and the cantrail centre band painted monaco green. The following month, Atlantean 22 was painted in a similar scheme but with large 'Rossendale' fleetnames in black lower case lettering above the skirt. This basic layout became the standard livery for a number of years, with single-deckers receiving a similar application with monaco green waistbands. There were many variations, and several batches of acquired vehicles carried different livery layouts within each batch. Some double-deckers didn't have the green cantrail band which was never applied to any of the Olympians. The use of green as a waistband or skirt lining was gradually phased out. Most MCW and Optare Metroriders had identical cream and red schemes with 'Handyrider' fleetnames. In later years, the cream areas were extended on these vehicles, whilst the 'Handyrider' branding was applied to most step-entrance Darts, including the Duple and Reeve-Burgess examples, which were painted white and red when new and were effectively the forerunners of the present 'Easyride' white, cream and red scheme that appeared in 1996 when the East Lancs Dart SLF's were launched and this has been the fleet standard for all low-floor vehicles to this day.

The rebranded Rossendale Coach Hire livery consisted of red and ivory with large fleetnames and this was also applied to coach seated double-deckers, 88 and 27; 88 being crimson lake from new but later repainted red and 27 receiving the red livery. Following the Ellen Smith purchase, all remaining coaches apart from the double-deckers and Leopard 81 were repainted into a revised version of the Ellen Smith livery with updated logos and renumbered into a common series. Evolution of coach liveries/branding after this time is beyond the scope of this publication.

This 1939 Leyland TS8c with Leyland body was formerly No. 50 in the Rawtenstall fleet. When new it was fitted with a Leyland torque convertor, hence the c suffix to the chassis designation, but this was replaced by a conventional clutch and gearbox whilst still in service. Withdrawn from service in 1957, it was then used as a mobile polling booth with three of its fellows, after which this one was purchased for preservation by Mr W Higgins of Chester and regularly attends rallies. It is shown in Whitehaven Bus Station in May 2003 when attending the Stagecoach Open Day and Rally at the West Cumbria Depot. *(HP)*

Preserved Haslingden No. 2, a Leyland PS1 with body by HV Burlingham of Blackpool, is shown at Kirkby Stephen in April 1999. The arrival of underfloor-engined chassis onto the market in the early 'fifties meant that buses such as this became redundant in many fleets as the opportunity was taken to dispense with conductors and initiate one-man-operation. *(BD)*

This preserved Haslingden Corporation East Lancashire-bodied Leyland PD2 is shown leaving the Piece Hall, Halifax, on Saturday 7th May 1995 after a successful Heart of the Pennines rally. It captures the spirit of the Haslingden double-decker perfectly. Number 14 was new in 1960 and was withdrawn from service in 1978. *(BD)*

Former Rawtenstall Corporation No. 58, an East Lancashire-bodied Leyland Tiger Cub, was photographed in Blackburn on Sunday 26th June 2000 with an ex-Blackburn Corporation East Lancashire bodied Leyland PD3 and a former Lancashire United Leyland Leopard following in the distance. *(BD)*

The real thing now, as Haslingden No. 11, a Leyland-bodied Leyland PD2 of 1953, shows off the attractive Haslingden blue and cream livery as it makes its way in service towards Accrington with hills in the background and the school warning sign prominent on the lamp post. Older readers will remember the torch sign warning of school children's presence. *(DP)*

This 1949 Leyland bodied PD2 was number 1 in the Rawtenstall fleet and retained this number when transferred to the Joint Committee fleet in 1968. Despite being at least 19 years old when photographed climbing to Rossendale Hospital, it was still looking very smart. The Rossendale fleetname is clearly visible and the maroon paintwork positively gleams in the sun. *(DP)*

The final vehicles purchased by Rawtenstall Corporation before the formation of the Joint Committee were Leyland PD3s with traditional exposed radiators. One of these, shown here, illustrates the classic lines of the East Lancashire body. Note that the stylish lettering adopted way back in 1931 with the Titan TD1s is still in use, and still looks smart and undated. *(DP)*

Ramsbottom No. 7, another of the Leyland PD3 fleet with East Lancashire body and dating from 1967, awaits its departure time from Rawtenstall before working to Bury. Leopard L1, FTB 650B and originally No. 50, waits its turn of duty at the rear of the bus station. *(DP)*

Rossendale No. 30, a 1964 Leyland PD3 with East Lancashire body, originally carrying the same number in the Rawtenstall fleet and dating from 1964, illustrates the Rossendale livery with cream window surrounds in Accrington. Alongside is Hyndburn No. 181 in the distinctive dark blue and red livery long associated with Accrington Corporation and later, Hyndburn Transport. *(DP)*

This 1981 view depicts an event that is unlikely to be repeated in the foreseeable future – a White Christmas and Christmas Day buses. Leyland Leopard 64 (ETC 664J) makes its way along Newchurch Road towards Waterfoot. A slightly longer journey than that of the photographer who travelled all of 12ft from home to capture the shot! *(JC)*

Of the numerous demonstration vehicles evaluated by Rossendale and its predecessors over the years, the one that evokes most comment is the articulated Leyland-DAB 'bendibus' that ran for a week at the end of March 1982. FHE 291V is seen here heading towards Bacup, pursued by far more conventional Leyland PD3 No. 46. *(JC)*

Leyland Titan operation finally came to a close on New Year's Eve, 1982, when the last two examples were retired. Their use on a local supermarket free bus service almost certainly prolonged their life here. Former Rawtenstall 39 (XTJ 939D) climbs up Cherry Tree Lane on its last day, heading towards Rawtenstall and still displaying evidence of its original livery in the gold lining below the upper deck cream band. *(JC)*

A view that typifies the Rossendale Transport operation in the late 1970s and early '80s; Bristol RE No. 6 (YTC 306N) operates a Bacup 'short' working evidenced by the absence of the 'via' destination, whilst Leyland PD3 39 (XTJ 939D) has run a works service from Water along the Lumb Valley and then heads towards Bacup on its way to Sharneyford for a school run. (JC)

The newest Leyland Leopard in the fleet prior to the arrival of the first 'proper' coaches was refurbished and fitted with coach seating in late 1982. Number 5 (WTJ 905L) received a special 'Rossendale Coach Hire' livery and was the first member of the fleet to venture overseas. It was rather closer to home when captured working the Waterfoot via Newchurch service in January 1983. (JC)

The first vehicle to receive an all-over advertising livery was Leyland Atlantean No. 17 (PTD 417S), which emerged in 1982 with a scheme promoting various Leisure Services for the Borough Council. The absence of a full destination display is due to it working a journey to Weir village, north of Bacup, to which operations had only recently begun, following the extensive service changes of mid-1982. (JC)

The recasting of services along the Bury, Bolton and Burnley corridors in June 1982 meant that Rossendale gained some workings on a revised Burnley-Bolton service, re-routed via Crawshawbooth and Loveclough and renumbered 273. The new destinations were simply added to the end of each blind and were hand painted. Atlantean No. 18 (STE 18S) in the original livery for the type is seen at Burnley Summit in August 1982 in an interesting post script to the saga of 50 years before, when the terminus of the Bury-Rawtenstall-Burnley service had to be curtailed only a few hundred yards away from the location of this view. (JC)

The final weekday of crew-operation in June 1982, as former Haslingden Leyland PD3 No. 46 (DTJ 960E) leads a convoy of vehicles along Haslingden Road out of Rawtenstall to take up service at one of the local Secondary schools. The photograph also captures a cross-section of the then current fleet as it has evolved over the years, with 1971 Leopard 63 and one of the 1980 Atlanteans also in view. *(JC)*

As bus deregulation loomed in late 1986, it was clear that Rossendale wouldn't have enough vehicles to cope with the amount of additional work that was awarded through the tendering process and several Leyland Leopards that had been stored as surplus the previous year were recertified for further service. The 1971 batch only ran for a few months until most of the ex Greater Manchester Fleetlines were prepared for service. 60 (ETC 660J) is working the Balladen service in March 1987 with evidence of recent snowfall clearly visible in the background around the Ski Rossendale complex. *(JC)*

The expansion of the fleet in the first few months following deregulation saw an influx of former Greater Manchester 'standard' double-deckers with Northern Counties bodywork, which, apart from a solitary wartime utility vehicle for Haslingden, were the first examples of this body make. Daimler Fleetline 41 (PRJ 497R) in the final version of the post 1982 double-deck livery, approaches Bacup town centre on its journey through the Mettle Cote Estate which, despite the service number, is actually a 464 working. *(JC)*

A number of initiatives have been launched over the years aimed at the weekend tourist. One such venture, introduced before the East Lancashire Railway extended passenger journeys back to Rawtenstall, was service 476 linking the Helmshore Textile Museum near Haslingden to the Railway Station at Ramsbottom. Bristol LHS No. 50 (SND 550X) is seen on Holcombe Road in August 1988. *(JC)*

With Rawtenstall Market and the hills of Cribden in the background, ex-Kelvin Scottish Leopard 74 (ULS 318T) collects its customers as it prepares to head along Newchurch Road towards Bacup. For many years, this 'Estates' service terminated at Britannia near Bacup, but in the 1980s it was extended to Bacup town centre and this particular working will continue on to Burnley. *(JC)*

There are some challenging climbs along some of the Valley's roads. Peel Street in Cloughfold, only ever served by vehicles on contract work or road testing, was the setting for this shot of newly repainted 21 (ABN 721V) in June 1989, working with two of its sisters in conjunction with an orienteering event being held nearby. *(JC)*

The use of route numbers on Rossendale buses was a relatively recent innovation and it was not until deregulation that their use became a necessity. In order to extend coverage on vehicles that had no suitable displays, a 'flip-over' type of arrangement was employed and retrofitted to a number of older single-deckers including the Bristol RE fleet. Number 14 (JDK 914P) demonstrates the application in this view at Newchurch in May 1991. *(JC)*

Number 10, a 1974 Bristol RE with East Lancashire bodywork, leaves Burnley Bus Station for Ski Rossendale in August 1991. Partially hidden behind the RE is an example of its somewhat contentious successor, the Leyland National, built at the erstwhile Workington plant in Cumbria. *(MB)*

When the first Carlyle-bodied Dennis Darts were delivered the Rossendale Company took the opportunity to photograph them for publicity purposes. The upper photograph shows No. 102 against the splendour of Rochdale Town Hall. The lower photograph shows numbers 101 and 102 at Ski Rossendale. *(RT)*

Also photographed against the background of Rochdale Town Hall is 1984-built Leyland Tiger A148 EPA, No. 89, fitted with Plaxton coach body and acquired from Kentish Bus in 1990.

Below: The terminus at Rossendale General Hospital affords some panoramic views of the part of the valley surrounding Rawtenstall town centre, which can be seen in the background. Former South Yorkshire PTE Alexander-bodied Atlantean 195 (JKW 295W), one of eight similar vehicles added to the fleet in 1991, prepares for its short trip back to town. There are no longer any scheduled services to the hospital, as the facility has been progressively run down over the last few years. *(JC)*

One of the last vehicles to be received by Rawtenstall before the amalgamation with Haslingden was this 1966 East Lancs-bodied Leyland PD3, number 39. It has been preserved, and is shown here in Rossendale livery at Pool In Wharfedale in August 1993, participating in the Trans Pennine Run. *(MB)*

The original Dennis Darts 101-3 were followed in 1991 by two further examples with Plaxton bodies, numbered 104/5, and the first of these is illustrated in Bury in August 1996 being followed by a Timeline vehicle. *(MB)*

MCW Metrorider number 67 is seen here in Rawtenstall operating the 13.30 Journey from Water to Balladen on Saturday 26th April 1997. *(BD)*

The A681 Bacup to Todmorden Road was served for many years by the green and cream Leylands of Todmorden Corporation before the route was abandoned in 1966. Whilst Ribble and Rawtenstall jointly worked replacement journeys as far as Sharneyford, it wasn't until after deregulation in 1986 that sporadic double-deck working to Todmorden could be observed. Atlantean No. 22 (ABN 722V) is seen in the autumn sunshine on the highest point of the route, and probably one of the highest double-deck worked routes in England. *(JC)*

Instantly recognisable body-styling confirms A741NNA is a 1984 Leyland Atlantean with bodywork by Northern Counties of Wigan to the GM Standard design and which was new to GM Buses. One of the last Atlanteans, built in 1984, it was purchased by Rossendale in 1997. It is shown in Rawtenstall in April 1999 heading for Balladen. *(MB)*

Number 121 was one of a batch of ten Dennis Dart SLF low-floor models with Plaxton bodies, purchased in 1998 for the Mainline 464 service between Accrington and Rochdale. It is shown employed on this service in Bacup in April 1999. *(MB)*

One of the Dennis Darts with Plaxton Pointer bodies hired to supplement existing similar vehicles on the 464 service in December 1999/January 2000 was S725 KNV. This view taken in Rochdale in May 2000 shows the route branding added to the plain white livery. *(RM)*

The very last Leylands to join the fleet came in the shape of a pair of Mark 1 Lynx that originated in the Brighton fleet, and whilst they saw some early use on the Mainline 464 service, such as No. 194 (G994 VWV) here in Waterfoot, for the majority of their time they were restricted to schools and peak-hour work. *(JC)*

Optare Metrorider number 54 was operating the 14.38 departure from Edenfield to Radcliffe when photographed at Ramsbottom in October 2001. *(BD)*

Heading out of Rawtenstall in September 2003 on service 483 to Bury is East Lancashire-bodied Dennis Dart No. 135 which was new in 2001. In addition to the Church, the tower of the fire station and the dome of the library can be seen behind the bus. *(RM)*

Rossendale provided some of the vehicles used for the Park and Ride service for the Commonwealth Games held at Sport City, Manchester, in 2002. East Lancashire-bodied Dennis Dart No. 141 is seen on 27th July. *(BD)*

In 1994 two new Volvo Olympians with Alexander 'Royale' bodies entered the fleet and were numbered 29 and 30. In August 2003, number 30 was loading at Blackburn Railway Station for the journey to Rochdale on service 244, a service which was operated for many years by Ribble. *(MB)*

Photographed in Accrington in August 2003 *en route* to Rochdale on Mainline service 464 is No. 145, one of eight Dennis Dart SLF models with East Lancashire 'Spryte' bodies purchased in 2002 specifically for this service. *(MB)*

Leaving Todmorden for Bacup on service 49 in August 2005 is Mercedes Sprinter number 2 with Koch body built in Germany. *(BD)*

Wright-bodied Volvo B7RLE No. 156 is shown working up the Rossendale Valley towards Bacup at the end of August 2006 whilst operating the Mainline service 464 from Accrington to Rochdale. Once again the route branded livery adds to the appearance of the bus. *(HP)*

The registration number R6 BLU identifies number 124 as one of four Plaxton-bodied Dennis Darts acquired from Blue Bus, Horwich, in 2002/3. It is shown in Rawtenstall bus station at the end of August, 2006. *(HP)*

The sleek lines of the Wright-bodied Volvo B7 are shown to good advantage in this March 2007 view taken in Bacup centre. An Optare Solo, YJ54 BUA, number 41, is bringing up the rear. *(HP)*

Number 166, a Dennis Dart SPD with Alexander body, one of four purchased from Munro's of Jedburgh in 2000, is descending the steep hill into Bacup in April 2007. *(HP)*

This splendidly-restored Leyland Tiger PS2, MTB 848 of 1950, number 55 in the Rawtenstall fleet, resides in the Manchester Museum of Transport along with Ramsbottom number 11, TTD 386H, the last traditional home-market front-engined double-decker bus. *(STA/JAS)*

The **Fleet Details** which follow have been supplied by John Cronshaw, to whom we extend our sincere thanks. John has also provided the following **Overview**

Before 1983, virtually all vehicles were new to the respective operators, with only a handful being pre-owned. The early 1980s witnessed a dramatic change in vehicle policy for many municipal operations with used vehicle purchases becoming the norm. The phasing out of New Bus Grant partly precipitated this along with a further decline in passenger numbers and revenue and the need to eliminate large financial deficits as operations such as Rossendale moved towards an era of deregulation and commercial independence from other council operations. For this reason and also to include as much detail as possible without confusing the reader, the fleet summaries are presented in a chronological format featuring the founding operations of Haslingden, Rawtenstall and Ramsbottom, followed by Rossendale JTC / Borough Transport and the Limited Company's fleet at the commencing of trading in the newly deregulated environment. Such was the pace of vehicle activity that followed from late 1986 to the present day, that the opportunity is taken to

present developments from this time in a slightly different and hopefully easier layout, identifying the source of the significant numbers of pre-owned stock coming into the fleet as well as the increasing trend in more recent years towards new vehicles.

The coaching operations are to be featured in a separate, future publication that will embrace the purchase of the Ellen Smith (Tours) business in 1991 and subsequent developments up to date. For this reason, full details of the vehicles that joined the fleet from Ellen Smith and all subsequent additions to the coach fleet are not included here. The situation is complicated by the fairly frequent number of transfers that took place between the two sides of the business, and we intend that this will capture the flavour of the complexities involved in two simultaneously expanding divisions of what was, a little over 20 years ago, just another modest municipally-owned bus operation, serving its local community and its near neighbours.

RAMSBOTTOM UDC FLEET DETAILS

No.	Registration	Chassis type	Body type and seating	Date In	Date Out	Notes
Trolleybus Fleet						
1-4	none	Railless Electric Traction	Milnes Voss B26R	1913	by 1931	a
5-6	none	Railless Electric Traction	L & C B26R	1915	1927-1928	b
7	unknown	Railless Limited	Short B26R	1922	1928	c
Motorbuses						
8	TC 780	Thornycroft J	Dodson B26R	1922	1927	
9	TC 4907	Thornycroft J	Roe B26D	1923	1924	d
10	TC 5979	Thornycroft J	Roe B26F	1924	1924	d
11	TC 7569	Thornycroft BT	Dodson B20F	1924	1933	e
10	TD 4886	Thornycroft A1	Hall Lewis B20F	1926	1931	f
13-14	TD 7539/40	Thornycroft A1	Roe B20F	1926	1929	
15-16	TD 8738/9	Leyland PLSC1	Leyland B31R	1927	1937	g
17	TE 1986	Leyland PLSC3	Leyland B35R	1927	1938	g
18	TE 4508	Leyland PLSC3	Leyland B35R	1928	1938	g
19	TE 6075	Leyland PLSC3	Roe B35R	1929	1946	g
20	TE 9253	Leyland LT1	Roe B31R	1929	1946	g
21	TE 9252	Leyland LT1	Leyland B30R	1929	1946	g
22	TF 3027	Leyland LT2	Roe B32R	1930	1946	g
23	TF 7112	Leyland LT5	Leyland B36R	1932	1946	g
12	TJ 2639	Leyland LT5	Roe B36R	1933	1950	h
10-11	TJ 7025/6	Leyland LT5A	Roe B36R	1934	1948-50	h
13-14	ATD 136/7	Leyland LT7	Roe B36R	1935	1950	h
8-9	CTB 138/9	Leyland TS7	Roe B36R	1937	1958, 1952	h
15	CTD 149	Leyland TS8	Roe B36R	1937	1958	h
6-7	ETD 52-53	Leyland TS8	Roe B36R	1939	1960	
16	GTC 975	Leyland PS1	Roe B35R	1946	1961	
17-19	HTB 656-658	Leyland PS1	Roe B35R	1947	1968, 1961/2	
20-25	HTF 815-20	Leyland PD2/1	Leyland H30/26R	1947	1965-69	i
26-28	MTC 255-7	Leyland PSU1/13	Roe B44F	1950	1962/3	j
29	MTC 998	Leyland PD2/1	Leyland H30/26R	1951	Selnec	
30	MTC 999	Leyland PSU1/13	Leyland B44F	1952	1966	
1	247 STD	Leyland PD2/24	East Lancs H35/28R	1961	Selnec	
2	367 XTE	Leyland PD2A/30	East Lancs H35/28R	1962	Selnec	
3	9459 TE	Leyland PD2A/30	East Lancs H35/28F	1963	Selnec	
4	LTD 232C	Leyland PD3A/1	East Lancs H41/32F	1965	Selnec	
5	TTB 879D	Leyland PD3A/1	East Lancs H41/32F	1966	Selnec	
6-7	DTC 415/6E	Leyland PD3/4	East Lancs H41/32F	1967	Selnec	
8-9	FTF 702/3F	Leyland PD3/4	East Lancs H41/32F	1967	Selnec	
12	RJX 258	Albion Nimbus NS3AN	Weymann B31F	1967	Selnec	k
10	OTJ 334G	Leyland PD3/14	East Lancs H41/32F	1969	Selnec	
11	TTD 386H	Leyland PD3/14	East Lancs H41/32F	1969	Selnec	l

Notes
- a. Rebodied Lockwood & Clarkson B28R between 1915-17. Later reseated B27R; 3 of the 4 were registered TB 8570-2 in 1921;
- b. Lockwood & Clarkson bodywork; Registered TB 8573 (1921) and TD 417 (1925).
- c. Registered TD 418 in 1925. Its original registration is unknown.
- d. 9 and 10 sold To Rawtenstall Corporation in 1924.
- e. The body make is thought to be Dodson, but hasn't been confirmed.
- f. 2 further Thornycroft A1 with unidentified B20F bodies are believed to have joined the fleet in 1926 but no precise details have emerged about these vehicles.
- g. 15-23 were renumbered 9, 8, 7, 6, 5, 4, 3, 2, 1 in 1932.
- h. 8-15 were modified to 35 seaters at a later date.
- i. 21was withdrawn in 1969 but was still in stock upon the formation of the SELNEC PTE in November 1969.
- j. 26 and 27 were sold to Rawtenstall and Haslingden Corporations, respectively in 1962.
  28 was sold to Haslingden Corporation in 1963.
- k. 12 was ex-Warrington 95 and was new in 1963 to Halifax Joint Omnibus Committee No. 258.
- l. 11 was the last traditional front-engined double-decker to enter service in the U.K. It did not enter service until after the formation of SELNEC PTE.

Selnec – denotes a vehicle transferred to SELNEC PTE from 1st November 1969

HASLINGDEN CTD FLEET DETAILS

No.	Registration	Chassis type	Body type and seating	Date In	Date Out	Notes
	B 2113	Leyland X	Leyland B20R	1907	1909	a
1	B 3455	BSA 14-18 h.p,	Heap B12F	1919	1920	
	TB 2518	Austin 2/3 ton	Barnes B22F	1920	1929	
1	TC 8581	Guy B	Guy B26F	1924	1932	
2	TD 4047	Guy BB	Guy B32D	1925	1933	b
3	TE 5736	Leyland PLC1	Davidson B28D	1928	1937	c
4	TE 9172	Leyland LT1	Leyland B31R	1929	1936	
5	TF 330	Leyland LT1	Leyland B31R	1930	1951	
6	TF 621	Leyland LT1	Leyland B31R	1930	1949	
7-8	TF1557-8	Leyland LT1	Leyland B31R	1930	1945, 1943	
9	TF 622	Leyland LT1	Leyland B31R	1930	1948	
10	TF 1559	Leyland LT1	Leyland B31R	1930	1942	
11	TF 2933	Leyland LT2	Leyland B31R	1930	1949	
12	TF 3845	Leyland LT2	Leyland B26D	1931	1949	
14-15	TF 7458, 7650	Leyland TD2	Leyland H24/24R	1932	1948	
16	TJ 885	Leyland TD2	Leyland H28/24R	1933	1950	
17	TJ 6999	Leyland TD3	Leyland H28/26R	1934	1950	
18-19	ATF 438-9	Leyland TD4	Leyland H30/26R	1936	1953, 1958	
20	CTD 747	Leyland TD5	Leyland H30/26R	1937	1960	
21	CTJ 540	Leyland TD5	Leyland H30/26R	1938	1960	
22	FTC 427	Guy Arab I 5LW	NCME L27/26R	1942	1952	
23	FTD 195	Daimler CWG5	Brush L27/28R	1943	1951	
24	FTE 768	Daimler CWA6	Brush H30/26R	1945	1955	
25	GTD 497	Leyland PD1	Alexander H30/26R	1946	1962	
26	HTC 833	Leyland PD1A	Leyland H30/26R	1947	1964	
27	JTJ 414	Leyland PD2/1	Leyland H30/26R	1948	1966	
1	JTJ 655	Leyland PS1	Burlingham B35F	1948	1966	
2	KTJ 502	Leyland PS1	Burlingham B35F	1949	1965	
3-4	KTJ 878-9	Leyland PS1	Burlingham B35F	1949	1964, RJTC	
6-7	MTC 385-6	Leyland PD2/1	Leyland H30/26R	1950	1966, RJTC	
8	NTD 530	Leyland PD2/1	Leyland H30/26R	1951	1968	
9	OTF 164	Leyland PD2/12	Leyland H30/26R	1953	RJTC	
10-11	PTF 207-8	Leyland PD2/12	Leyland H30/26R	1953	RJTC	
5	TTB 302	Leyland PD2/12	East Lancs H31/28R	1954	RJTC	
12	VTJ 90	Leyland PD2/12	East Lancs H31/28R	1955	RJTC	
13	11 CTB	Leyland PD2/12	East Lancs H31/28R	1957	RJTC	
14	192 OTB	Leyland PD2/40	East Lancs H31/28R	1960	RJTC	
15-16	MTC 256-7	Leyland PSU1/13	Roe B44F	1962/3	RJTC	
17	FTF 732B	Leyland L1	East Lancs B44F	1964	RJTC	
18	NTJ 808C	Leyland L1	East Lancs B44F	1965	RJTC	
—	WTC 763D	Morris J2BM	Morris M11	1966	RJTC	
1	XTF 98D	Leyland PD3/4	East Lancs H41/32F	1966	RJTC	
2	DTJ 960E	Leyland PD3/14	East Lancs H41/32F	1967	RJTC	

Notes

a. Used as a tower wagon after withdrawal until 1925.
b. Also reported as B32F
c. Also quoted as having a Leyland B28F body.
RJTC Nos. 1, 2, 4, 5, 7, 9-18 and WTC 763D (a total of 16 vehicles) were transferred to Rossendale Joint Transport Committee on 1/4/68. Vehicle numbers 4, 15 & 16 were not used.

RAWTENSTALL CM BUS FLEET DETAILS

No.	Registration	Chassis type	Body type and seating	Date In	Date Out	Notes
	FA 157, 159	Ryknield 40/50 h.p.	unidentified O—/—RO	1907/8	1910	a
33-36	TC 9001-4	Leyland SG9	Leyland B40D	1924	1931/3	
37-38	TC 9690-1	Leyland SG9	Leyland B40D	1924	1931/3	
39-40	TC 4907, 5979	Thornycroft J	Roe B26D, B26F	1924	1930	b
41-42	TD 2950/1	Leyland SG11	Leyland B36D	1925	1933	
43-44	TD 8678/9	Leyland PLSC1	Leyland B31R	1927	1937, 1934	
45-46	TD 8926/7	Leyland PLSC1	Leyland B29F	1927	1937, 1934	c
47-48	TF 1099, 1181	Leyland TS2	Leyland B30R	1930	1940, 1939	
49-52	TF 1182-5	Leyland LT1	Leyland B30R	1930	1938	
53-54	TF 4236/7	Leyland TD1	Leyland H27/24R	1931	1945, 1947/8	
55-57	TF 6081/2, 6856	Leyland TD1	Leyland H27/24R	1931	1946-8	
58-59	TF 6857/8	Leyland TS1	Leyland B30R	1931	1939	
60-62	TF 6859-61	Leyland LT3	Leyland B36R	1931	1940-48	d
1-10	TF 7894-7903	Leyland TD2	Leyland H27/24R	1932	1948/9	
11-12	TF 8372/3	Leyland TD2	Leyland H27/24R	1932	1948	
13-14	TF 9180/1	Leyland TD2	Leyland H27/24R	1932	1948, 1947	
15-16	TJ 569/70	Leyland TD2	Leyland H30/24R	1933	1943/7	
17-18	TJ 2468/9	Leyland TD3	Leyland H30/24R	1932	1953, 1952	e
19-20	TJ 6673/4	Leyland TD3c	Leyland H30/24R	1934	1949/50	
21-22	ATC 121/2	Leyland TD4	Leyland H28/26R	1935	1955	f
23-24	BTB 19, 20	Leyland TD4	Leyland H30/26R	1936	1953	
25	BTB 119	Leyland TD4c	Leyland H30/24R	1936	1953	
26	BTB 120	Leyland TD4	Leyland H30/36R	1936	1953	
27-28	CTB 713/4	Leyland TD5c	Leyland H30/24R	1937	1956, 1955	
29-34	CTJ 161-6	Leyland TD5c	Leyland H30/24R	1938	1955-1958	
45-46	DTD 249/50	Leyland TS8c	Leyland B36R	1938	1957, 1953	g
35-36	DTJ 56/7	Leyland TD5c	Leyland H30/25R	1939	1959	
50-52	DTJ 58-60	Leyland TS8c	Leyland B36R	1939	1954-1960	g
37	FTD 450	Guy Arab II 6LW	Massey H30/26R	1943	1964	h
38-40	GTD 501-3	Leyland PD1A	Alexander H30/26R	1947	1964	
41-44	HTF 361-4	Leyland PD2/1	Leyland H30/26R	1947	1965/6, RJTC	
47-49	HTF 365-7	Leyland PD2/1	Leyland H30/26R	1947	1966	
11-14	JTE 496-9	Leyland PD2/1	East Lancs H30/26R	1948	1962-5	
15	JTJ 568	Leyland PD2/1	East Lancs H30/26R	1948	1966	
53-54	KTD 755/6	Leyland PS1	East Lancs B34R	1949	1964, 1963	i
1-10	KTE 721-30	Leyland PD2/1	Leyland H30/26R	1949	RJTC	
55-56	MTB 848/9	Leyland PS2/1	East Lancs B35R	1950	RJTC	d
16	NTD 529	Leyland PD2/1	Leyland H30/26R	1951	RJTC	
17-19	RTC 821-3	Leyland PD2/12	Leyland H31/25R	1953	RJTC	
20/4-6	RTE 534-7	Leyland PD2/12	East Lancs H31/28R	1953	RJTC	j
60-65	VTJ 731-6	Leyland PD2/20	East Lancs H31/28R	1955	RJTC	j
57	RTB 49	Leyland PSUC1/1	Weymann B44F	1955	RJTC	k
58	466 FTJ	Leyland PSUC1/5	East Lancs B43F	1958	RJTC	
59	738 NTD	Leyland PSUC1/5	East Lancs B43F	1960	RJTC	
—	1386 TF	Austin J2BA	Austin M11	1963	RJTC	
52	MTC 255	Leyland PSU1/13	Roe B44F	1963	RJTC	l
30-33	FTE 630-3B	Leyland PD3/4	East Lancs H41/32F	1964	RJTC	
50-51	FTE 650/1B	Leyland L1	East Lancs B44F	1964	RJTC	
34-37	MTJ 434-7C	Leyland PD3/4	East Lancs H41/32F	1965	RJTC	
38-41	XTJ 938-41D	Leyland PD3/4	East Lancs H41/32F	1966	RJTC	

Notes

a.	FA 157 used as a tower wagon after withdrawal until c1932.
b.	Ex-Ramsbottom UDC 9, 10 and new 1923 and 1924, respectively
c.	Renumbered 39 and 40 in 1930.
d.	61 (TF 6860) and 55 (MTB 848) were used as towing vehicles after withdrawal.
e.	Rebodied NCB H30/26R in 1944 and 1945, respectively.
f.	Rebodied Burlingham H30/26R in 1946 and 1947, respectively.
g.	45, 46, 50 and 52 were converted to mobile polling booths for use in Council elections.
h.	Rebodied East Lancs H30/26R in 1951.
i.	53 and 54 had East Lancs (Bridlington) bodywork.
j.	24-26, 60-65 were renumbered 21-29 in January 1964.
k.	Ex-Leyland Motors demonstrator, new in 1953 . Body originally fitted to demonstrator OTD 301.
l.	Ex-Ramsbottom UDC No. 26. New 1950.
RJTC	Nos. 1-10, 16-42, 50-52, 55-9 and 1386 TF (a total of 46 vehicles) were transferred to Rossendale Joint Transport Committee on 1/4/68. 42, 52, 55 and 56 were not used.

ROSSENDALE JTC / BOROUGH COUNCIL
FLEET DETAILS

No.	Registration	Chassis type	Body type and seating	Date In	Date Out	Notes
Former Haslingden & Rawtenstall vehicles - operational						
1-10	KTE 721-30	Leyland PD2/1	Leyland H30/26R	1949	1970-3	
11	MTC 385	Leyland PD2/1	Leyland H30/26R	1950	1970	
12	OTF 164	Leyland PD2/12	Leyland H30/26R	1953	1968	
13-14	PTF 207-8	Leyland PD2/12	Leyland H30/26R	1953	1972/3	
15	TTB 302	Leyland PD2/12	East Lancs H31/28R	1954	1973	
16	NTD 529	Leyland PD2/1	Leyland H30/26R	1951	1971	
17-19	RTC 821-3	Leyland PD2/12	Leyland H31/25R	1953	1973/4	
20-23	RTE 534-7	Leyland PD2/12	East Lancs H31/28R	1953	1969-74	
24-29	VTJ 731-6	Leyland PD2/20	East Lancs H31/28R	1955	1971-77	
30-33	FTE 630-3B	Leyland PD3/4	East Lancs H41/32F	1964	1977-82	
34-37	MTJ 434-7C	Leyland PD3/4	East Lancs H41/32F	1965	1978-82	
38-41	XTJ 938-41D	Leyland PD3/4	East Lancs H41/32F	1966	1979-82	
42	VTJ 90	Leyland PD2/12	East Lancs H31/28R	1955	1974	
43	11 CTB	Leyland PD2/12	East Lancs H31/28R	1957	1974	
44	192 OTB	Leyland PD2/40	East Lancs H31/28R	1960	1978	a
45	XTF 98D	Leyland PD3/4	East Lancs H41/32F	1966	1982	
46	DTJ 960E	Leyland PD3/14	East Lancs H41/32F	1967	1982	
48	FTF 732B	Leyland L1	East Lancs B44F	1964	1980	b
49	NTJ 808C	Leyland L1	East Lancs B44F	1965	1981	
50-51	FTE 650/1B	Leyland L1	East Lancs B44F	1964	1981	
57	RTB 49	Leyland PSUC1/1	Weymann B44F	1955	1971	
58	466 FTJ	Leyland PSUC1/5	East Lancs B43F	1958	1979	
59	738 NTD	Leyland PSUC1/5	East Lancs B43F	1960	1978	
—	1386 TF	Austin J2BA	Austin M11	1963	1969	
—	WTC 763D	Morris J2BM	Morris M11	1966	1972	
Former Haslingden & Rawtenstall vehicles – not used or withdrawn at the date of transfer						
4	KTJ 879	Leyland PS1	Burlingham B35F	1949	—	
15-16	MTC 256-7	Leyland PSU1/13	Roe B44F	1962/3	—	
42	HTF 362	Leyland PD2/1	Leyland H30/26R	1947	—	
52	MTC 255	Leyland PSU1/13	Roe B44F	1963	—	
55-56	MTB 848/9	Leyland PS2/1	East Lancs B35R	1950	—	b
New Vehicles purchased by the JTC and Borough Council						
52-54	JTF 152-4F	Leyland PSU4/2R	East Lancs B44F	1968	1982, 1984	c
55-56	LTD 955/6F	Leyland PSU4/2R	East Lancs B46F	1968	1985	d
60-65	ETC 660-5J	Leyland PSU4A/2R	East Lancs B46F	1971	RTL	e
66-70	MTC 866-70K	Leyland PSU4B/2R	East Lancs B46F	1972	1985, RTL	f
1-5	WTJ 901-5L	Leyland PSU4B/2R	East Lancs B45F	1973	RTL	g
6-10	YTC 306-10N	Bristol RESL6L	East Lancs B46F	1974	RTL	
11-12	JDK 911/2P	Bristol RESL6L	East Lancs DP42F	1975	RTL	
13-14	JDK 913/4P	Bristol RESL6L	East Lancs B45F	1975	RTL	
15-17	PTD 415-7S	Leyland AN68A/1R	East Lancs H43/32F	1977	RTL	
18-19	STE 18, 19S	Leyland AN68A/1R	East Lancs H43/32F	1978	RTL	
20	VTD 720T	Leyland AN68A/1R	East Lancs H43/32F	1979	RTL	
21-23	ABN 721-3V	Leyland AN68A/1R	East Lancs H43/32F	1979	RTL	
24-26	DDK 24-26W	Leyland AN68B/1R	East Lancs H43/32F	1980	RTL	
27-28	SND 27, 28X	Leyland AN68C/1R	East Lancs H43/32F	1982	RTL	h
50-51	SND 550/1X	Bristol LHS6L	East Lancs B28F	1982	RTL	

ROSSENDALE JTC / BOROUGH COUNCIL
FLEET DETAILS continued

No.	Registration	Chassis type	Body type and seating	Date In	Date Out	Notes

Used vehicles purchased by the Borough Council

No.	Registration	Chassis type	Body type and seating	Date In	Date Out	Notes
'18'	RTC 822	Leyland PD2/12	Leyland H31/25R	1982	RTL	i
52	TPJ 56S	Bristol LHS6L	ECW B34F	1983	RTL	j
29	HGG 243N	Leyland AN68/1R	Alexander H45/31F	1984	RTL	k
30	JUS 795N	Leyland AN68/1R	Alexander H45/31F	1984	RTL	k
31	KSU 857P	Leyland AN68A/1R	Alexander H45/31F	1984	RTL	k
80	DKG 272V	Leyland PSU3F/5R	Plaxton C53F	1985	RTL	l
81-82	GBO 243/5W	Leyland PSU3F/5R	Plaxton C53F	1985	RTL	l
83-84	NDW 149/8X	Leyland TRCTL11/2R	Plaxton C53F	1986	RTL	l
175	CTC 175J	Leyland PDR1A/1	East Lancs H45/33F	1986	RTL	m
176/9	HTF 176/9K	Leyland PDR1A/1	East Lancs H45/33F	1986	RTL	m

Notes

Refer to the Haslingden & Rawtenstall sections for additional information on the vehicles that were transferred to Rossendale Joint Transport Committee.

a. Converted to permanent driver training vehicle and transferred to Rossendale Transport Limited in October 1986.

b. 48 and 55 converted to towing vehicles after withdrawal. 48 replaced 55 in this role and was transferred to Rossendale Transport Limited in October 1986.

c. Ordered by Rawtenstall Corporation but delivered to Rossendale JTC.

d. Ordered by Haslingden Corporation but delivered to Rossendale JTC.

e. 60, 63 and 65 had been withdrawn at the time of the transfer to Rossendale Transport Limited but were placed back in service as soon as the limited company began trading.

f. 67 and 69 were withdrawn at the time of transfer to Rossendale Transport Limited and were not used by the limited company.

g. 1 and 3 were later reseated to B35F (1982 and 1983), whilst 5 was fitted with coach seating in 1982 and reclassified as DP43F.

h. 27 was rebuilt to CH43/27F in October 1986 by East Lancs (coach seating fitted).

i. '18' was re-purchased having previously been operated from 1953 to 1974. It had been in preservation with Gerald Walker of Tower Coaches, Wigton since 1976 and was used by Rossendale as a preserved vehicle. From 1986 it was also used as an additional driver training vehicle.

j. 52 was formerly London Country Bus Services No. BN56 and was new in 1977 as B35F.

k. 29-31 were formerly Strathclyde PTE Nos. LA894, LA948 and LA981 and were new in 1975.

l. 80-84 were formerly Hills of Tredegar and were new in 1980 (80), 1981 (81 and 82) or 1982 (83 and 84).

m. 175, 176 and 179 were formerly Hyndburn Transport Nos. 175, 186 and 179 and were new in 1971. They were not operated in service by Rossendale Borough Transport and were first used after the limited company began to trade.

RTL Denotes a vehicle or batch of vehicles that were transferred to Rossendale Transport Limited in October 1986.

ROSSENDALE TRANSPORT LIMITED

Vehicles acquired by Rossendale Transport Limited from October 1986 to Date

No.	Registration	Chassis type	Body type and seating	New
53-55	D953-5 NOJ	Freight-Rover Sherpa	Carlyle / Dormobile DP20F	1986
71	JDK 921P	Leyland PSU3C/4R	Plaxton B44D	1975
72	JDK 925P	Leyland PSU4C/4R	Plaxton B44F	1975
35-38	OBN 502-5/7R	Leyland FE30AGR	NCME H43/32F	1977
39-41	PRJ 485/96/7R	Daimler CRG6LXB	NCME H43/32F	1976
42-43	YNA 341/56M	Daimler CRG6LXB	NCME H43/32F	1974
88	D888 YHG	Leyland ONTL11/2RH	East Lancs CH47/31F	1987
78	WCK 123V	Leyland PSU3E/4R	Duple C49F	1979
79	GRF 268V	Leyland PSU3E/4R	Duple C53F	1980
44-45	GND 500/3N	Daimler CRG6LXB	NCME H43/32F	1974
—	NHL 532F	Leyland PSU3A/4R	Plaxton DP—F	1968
73-74	ULS 316/8T	Leyland PSU3E/4R	Alexander B53F	1979
75-76	ULS 322/34T	Leyland PSU3E/4R	Alexander B53F	1979
—	XTJ 939D	Leyland PD3/4	East Lancs H41/32F	1966
56-59	E56-59 KHG	MCW MF151/8	MCW B23F	1988
80	B66 YFV	Leyland TRCTL11/3RZ	Plaxton C49FT	1985
99	OGE 9Y	Leyland TRCTL11/2R	Duple B55F	1983
96	A196 WGE	Leyland TRCTL11/2R	Duple B51F	1984
118-120	BAJ 118-20Y	Leyland TRCTL11/2R	Duple B55F	1983
92	F92 XBV	Leyland TRBTL11/2RP	East Lancs DP49F	1989
93-95	F93-95 XBV	Leyland TRBTL11/2RP	East Lancs B51F	1989
60-62	F60-62 ARN	MCW MF150/106	MCW B25F	1989
63	F63 ARN	MCW MF150/120	MCW B25F	1989
162-164	PHB 362-4R	Leyland PSU4D/2R	Duple B47F	1977
'174'	CWT 474H	Leyland PSU3A/4R	Willowbrook DP49F	1969
64	E519 YWF	MCW MF150/35	MCW B25F	1987
128-131	VDY 528-31T	Leyland AN68A/2R	East Lancs H47/35F	1978
136-137	CJK 36-37V	Leyland AN68B/1R	East Lancs H43/31F	1980
67	E674 DCU	MCW MF150/62	MCW B21F	1987
85	A110 EPA	Leyland TRCTL11/2RH	Plaxton C53F	1983
87	A133 EPA	Leyland TRCTL11/2RH	Plaxton C53F	1984
46	RJA 705R	Leyland AN68A/1R	NCME H43/32F	1977
47	SRJ 740R	Leyland AN68A/1R	NCME H43/32F	1977
48-49	ONF 684/92R	Leyland AN68A/1R	NCME H43/32F	1976/7
89	A148 EPA	Leyland TRCTL11/3R	Plaxton C51F	1984
90	D741 ALR	MCW MF150/6	MCW C16F	1987
101-103	H101-3 VFV	Dennis Dart	Duple B36F	1990
127	WEX 827X	Leyland PSU3G/4R	ECW C47F	1982
176	XPW 876X	Leyland PSU3G/4R	ECW C47F	1982
154	CWG 754V	Leyland AN68A/1R	Roe H45/33F	1979
188	JKW 288W	Leyland AN68B/1R	Alexander H45/33F	1981
190/1	JKW 290/1W	Leyland AN68B/1R	Alexander H45/33F	1981
193-197	JKW 293-7W	Leyland AN68B/1R	Alexander H45/33F	1981
104-105	H104/5 CHG	Dennis Dart	Reeve-Burgess B35F	1991
—	CWG 722V	Leyland AN68A/1R	Alexander H—/—D	1980
183	JNH 183Y	Leyland PSU3G/4R	ECW C46F	1983
1-4	F91-94 CWG	MCW MF150/105	MCW B23F	1988
9	D859 LND	Dodge S56	N.C.M.E. B20F	1986
10	D901 MDB	Dodge S56	N.C.M.E. B20F	1987
5	D21 CFL	MCW MF150/23	MCW DP25F	1987
8	E248 UWR	MCW MF150/80	MCW B23F	1988
75	WCK 139V	Leyland PSU3E/4R	Duple C—F	1980

ROSSENDALE TRANSPORT LIMITED

Date In	Date Out	Former Operator	Notes
1986	1993/4	new	a
1986	1988	Greater Manchester PTE	
1986	1993	Greater Manchester PTE	
1987	1992	Greater Manchester PTE	
1987	1992	Greater Manchester PTE	
1987	1990/1	Greater Manchester PTE	
1987	1995	new	b
1987	rebodied	Ribble Motor Services	
1987	rebodied	Barry Cooper, Stockton Heath	
1987	1991/2	Greater Manchester PTE	
1987	—	Border Tours, Barnoldswick	spares only
1987	1993	Kelvin Scottish Omnibuses	
1987	1993	Kelvin Scottish Omnibuses	
1988	1992	Rossendale Borough Transport	ex preservation
1988	1995-98	new	
1988	1996	Ribble Motor Services	
1988	1999	Hutchison, Overtown	
1988	1999	Hutchison, Overtown	
1988	1999	Trimdon Motor Services	
1989	2000	new	
1989	2000	new	
1989	1998	new	
1989	1998	new	
1989	rebodied / 1993	Inter Valley Link	c
1989	—	Border Tours, Barnoldswick	spares only
1989	1998	Avon, Prenton	
1989	1997/8	Hastings Topline Buses	d
1989	1998	Hastings Topline Buses	d
1990	1999	Moor-Dale, Newcastle	
1990	1993	Kentish Bus	
1990	EST	Kentish Bus	EST
1990	1997	Greater Manchester Buses	
1990	1997	Greater Manchester Buses	
1990	1998, 1997	Greater Manchester Buses	
1990	EST	Kentish Bus	EST
1990	EST	Capital Coaches, West Drayton	EST
1990	2004/5	new	
1990	1994	Ambassador Travel (Anglia) Ltd	
1990	1994	Ambassador Travel (Anglia) Ltd	
1991	1994	South Yorkshire PTE	ex H45/29D
1991	1998	South Yorkshire PTE	ex H45/29D
1991	1998	South Yorkshire PTE	ex H45/29D
1991	1993-98	South Yorkshire PTE	ex H45/29D
1991	2004	new	
1991	—	South Yorkshire PTE	spares only
1991	1995	Border, Burnley	
1991	1999	Bee Line Buzz Co.	
1992	1997	Evans, Tregaron	e
1992	1997	Greater Manchester Buses	
1992	1997	Robinson, Kimbolton	
1993	1999	Yorkshire Rider	
1993	rebodied	Blue Bus, Horwich	f

ROSSENDALE TRANSPORT LIMITED

No.	Registration	Chassis type	Body type and seating	New
64-65	F164/5 DET	MCW MF150/120	MCW B25F	1989
67	F171 DET	MCW MF150/106	MCW B25F	1989
68-69	F168/9 DET	MCW MF150/120	MCW B25F	1989
31-32	B101/2 PHC	Leyland ONLXCT/2R	East Lancs H47/35F	1985
76	VAJ 784S	Leyland PSU3E/4R	East Lancs (rebody) B51F	1977
11-12	L911/2 ECW	Optare Metrorider MR09	Optare B23F	1993
13-14	L813/4 KCW	Optare Metrorider MR31	Optare B25F	1994
—	BNE 756N	Leyland AN68/1R	NCME H—/—F	1974
29-30	M529/30 RHG	Volvo YN2RV18Z4	Alexander H43/29F	1994
199	E764 KJX	Talbot Freeway	Talbot B16FL	1988
52-53	E481/3 CNM	MCW MF150/72	MCW B23F	1988
54-55	E979/80 DGS	MCW MF150/72	MCW B23F	1988
66	E977 DGS	MCW MF150/72	MCW B23F	1988
45	D601 AFR	MCW MF151/4	MCW B23F	1987
41-42	F111/5 YWO	MCW MF150/103	MCW DP23F	1988
43-44	E143/4 KYW	MCW MF150/38	MCW B23F	1987
39-40	F103/13 YWO	MCW MF150/103	MCW DP23F	1988
106-110	N106-10 LCK	Dennis Dart SLF	East Lancs B28F	1996
132	ANA 217T	Leyland AN68A/1R	NCME H43/32F	1978
133	FVR 259V	Leyland AN68A/1R	NCME H43/32F	1979
134	MNC 521W	Leyland AN68A/1R	NCME H43/32F	1980
73	NCS 117W	Volvo B10M-61	East Lancs (rebody) B51F	1981
74	BSG 551W	Leyland TRCTL11/3R	East Lancs (rebody) B53F	1981
98	D376 RHS	Volvo B10M-61	Duple B55F	1987
135	ANA 585Y	Leyland AN68D/1R	NCME H43/32F	1982
138	SND 418X	Leyland AN68A/1R	NCME H43/32F	1981
15-16	P915/6 XUG	Optare Metrorider MR31	Optare B25F	1997
111-113	P211-3 DCK	Dennis Dart SLF	East Lancs B28F	1997
17	H117 MOB	Dennis Dart	Carlyle B28F	1990
18	H611 MOM	Dennis Dart	Carlyle B28F	1990
19	H119 MOB	Dennis Dart	Carlyle B28F	1990
20-21	H620/1 MOM	Dennis Dart	Carlyle B28F	1990
81-83	H102/4/9 MOB	Dennis Dart	Carlyle B28F	1990
84-86	H120/12/4 MOB	Dennis Dart	Carlyle B28F	1990
87-91	H127-31 MOB	Dennis Dart	Carlyle B28F	1990/1
72	PJI 9172	Leyland PSU3G/4R	ECW C53F	1983
33	B183 FDM	Volvo B10M-50	East Lancs CH45/33F	1985
51	NSU 181	MCW MF150/9	MCW DP25F	1987
130/1	A752/41 NNA	Leyland AN68D/1R	NCME H43/32F	1984
68-69	F338/9 VSD	Volvo B10M-56	Duple B53F	1988
126-127	L26-27 FNE	Dennis Dart	Marshall B40F	1994
128-129	K28-29 XBA	Dennis Dart	Marshall B40F	1993/2
22-23	H108/10 MOB	Dennis Dart	Carlyle B28F	1990
24-26	H113/5/6 MOB	Dennis Dart	Carlyle B28F	1990
80	H118 MOB	Dennis Dart	Carlyle B28F	1990
139-140	C39-40 CHM	Leyland ONLXB/1RH	ECW H42/30F	1986
141/3	C34, 93 CHM	Leyland ONLXB/1RH	ECW H42/30F	1986
144-145	C84-85 CHM	Leyland ONLXB/1RH	ECW H42/30F	1986
146	C96 CHM	Leyland ONLXB/1RH	ECW H42/30F	1986
148-150	C88-90 CHM	Leyland ONLXB/1RH	ECW H42/30F	1986
114-123	S114-23 KRN	Dennis Dart SPD	Plaxton B40F	1998
54/7-9	J584/7-9 CUB	Optare Metrorider MR07	Optare DP25F	1992
34	G304 UYK	Leyland ONCL10/1RZ	Leyland H47/31F	1989
35	G307 UYK	Leyland ON2R50C13Z4	Leyland H47/31F	1989
36	G312 UYK	Leyland ON2R50C13Z4	Leyland H47/29F	1989
37-38	G313/4 UYK	Leyland ON2R50C13Z4	Leyland CH43/29F	1989

ROSSENDALE TRANSPORT LIMITED

Date In	Date Out	Former Operator	Notes
1993	1999	Liverbus	
1993	1999	Liverbus	
1993	1997/99	Liverbus	
1993	2000	Stevensons	g
1993	2003	South Lancs Transport, St Helens	
1993	2004	new	
1994	2005	new	
1994	—	Nottinghamshire County Council	spares only
1994		new	
1995	2000	Employment Service, Sheffield	
1995	1997/98	Sovereign Bus & Coach	
1995	1998	Sovereign Bus & Coach	
1995	1997	Welwyn & Hatfield Line	
1995	1997	Blackburn Borough Transport	
1995	1997/99	Rhondda Buses	
1995	1997/98	Rhondda Buses	
1996	1997/98	Rhondda Buses	
1996		new	
1996	1998	Greater Manchester Buses South	
1996	2000	Greater Manchester Buses South	
1996	2001	Greater Manchester Buses South	
1997	2003	Allander Travel, Milngavie	
1997	2002	Allander Travel, Milngavie	
1997	2003	Allander Travel, Milngavie	
1997	1998	Greater Manchester Buses South	
1997	1998	Greater Manchester Buses South	
1997	2005	new	
1997		new	
1997	2004	Metroline Travel	
1997	2004	Metroline Travel	
1997	2004	Metroline Travel	
1997	2002, 2001	Metroline Travel	
1997	2004/5	Metroline Travel	
1997	2004/5	Metroline Travel	
1997	2004/5	Metroline Travel	
1997	1999	Border, Burnley	h
1997	2000	Ellen Smith	i
1997	2000	Ellen Smith	j
1997	2001	Greater Manchester Buses South	
1997	2004	Hutchison, Overtown	
1998		Mayne, Clayton	
1998		Mayne, Clayton	
1998	2003	Metroline Travel	
1998	2003	Metroline Travel	
1998	2003	Metroline Travel	
1998	2004	London Central	Ex H42/26D
1998	2004	London Central	Ex H42/26D
1998	2004	London Central	Ex H42/26D
1998	2004	London Central	Ex H42/26D
1998	2004	London Central	Ex H42/26D
1998		new	
1999	2002/4	APCOA, Sunbury	
1999		London United Busways	
1999		London United Busways	
1999		London United Busways	
1999		London United Busways	

ROSSENDALE TRANSPORT LIMITED

No.	Registration	Chassis type	Body type and seating	New
144-145	S724/5 KNV	Dennis Dart SLF	Plaxton B39F	1998
147	S377 TMB	Dennis Dart SLF	Plaxton B39F	1998
177-186	H177-86 OSG	Leyland LX2R11C15Z4S	Leyland B47F	1991
199	N352 BKK	Mercedes-Benz 709D	Plaxton DP16FL	1996
131-134	X131-4 JCW	Dennis Dart SPD	Plaxton B40F	2000
194/6	G994/6 VWV	Leyland LX112L10ZR1	Leyland B47F	1990
215	G915 UPP	Mercedes-Benz 709D	Reeve Burgess B23F	1989
382	VOY 182X	Leyland TRCTL/2R	Plaxton C53F	1981
135	PO 51 WEC	Dennis Dart SLF	East Lancs B37F	2001
136-137	PF 51 KMM/O	Dennis Dart SLF	East Lancs B37F	2002
138-140	PF 51 KMU/V/X	Dennis Dart SLF	East Lancs B37F	2002
141-142	PF 02 XMX/W	Dennis Super Dart	East Lancs B41F	2002
143-145	PN 52 WWK-M	Dennis Super Dart	East Lancs B41F	2002
146-148	PN 52 WWO/P/R	Dennis Super Dart	East Lancs B41F	2002
124-125	R6-7 BLU	Dennis Dart SLF	Plaxton B36F	1998
130	R8 BLU	Dennis Dart SLF	Plaxton B36F	1998
149	S9 BLU	Dennis Dart SLF	Plaxton B36F	1998
150	PO 53 OBU	Volvo B7RLE	Wright B44F	2003
151-153	PO 53 OBM/N/P	Volvo B7RLE	Wright B44F	2003
154-155	PO 53 OBR/T	Volvo B7RLE	Wright B44F	2003
156	PJ 53 UHV	Volvo B7RLE	Wright B44F	2003
157	BX 03 BKU	Volvo B7RLE	Wright B44F	2003
19-26	S859-66 DGX	Volvo Olympian OLY-50	NCME H47/29F	1998
1-3	BX 04 MZU-W	Mercedes-Benz 411CDI	Koch M15	2004
4	BX 04 MZZ	Mercedes-Benz 411CDI	Koch M15	2004
66-67	G728/7 JJC	Volvo B10M-55	Plaxton DP53F	1989
41-43	YJ 54 BUA/E/F	Optare Solo M880	Optare B25F	2004
44-46	YJ 54 BUH/O/P	Optare Solo M880	Optare B25F	2004
47-49	YJ 54 BUU-W	Optare Solo M880	Optare B25F	2004
50-53	YJ 54 UXT-W	Optare Solo M880	Optare B25F	2005
54-58	YJ 05 JWC-G	Optare Solo M880	Optare B25F	2005
59-63	YJ 05 JWK-O	Optare Solo M880	Optare B25F	2005
158	CU 04 AMX	MAN 14.220	MCV B39F	2004
159	CU 04 AOP	MAN 14.220	MCV B39F	2004
160	CU 04 AUV	MAN 14.220	MCV B39F	2004
10	R410 XFL	Dennis Dart SLF	Marshall B39F	1997
12	R712 MEW	Dennis Dart SLF	Marshall B39F	1998
163-166	X463-6 UKS	Dennis Dart SPD	Alexander B43F	2000

Notes

a. Ordered by Rossendale Borough Transport; Fitted with Dormobile van shells, converted by Carlyle.

b. Ordered by Rossendale Borough Transport; transferred to the Ellen Smith operation from 1992-94 as No. 388.

c. Purchased from National Welsh Omnibus Services, but last operated by Inter Valley Link.

d. New to Eastbourne Borough Council, from whom the vehicles were purchased.

e. New to Greater Manchester Buses.

f. New to Ribble and purchased as a seatless shell for removal of the bodywork and subsequent rebodying.

g. New to Eastbourne Borough Council.

h. Operated from 1991 to 1995 as 183, 75 and later as 72.

i. Purchased in 1993 from Wright, Wrexham for the Ellen Smith fleet as 393 and renumbered 33 when transferred to normal bus duties.

j. Purchased in 1992 from the Patrick Collection, Birmingham as 392, registered D87 EDH and used in the Ellen Smith fleet. It was re-registered to NSU 181 in 1993.

k. Owned by Lancashire County Council.

l. Purchased in 1999 from Goodwin, Eccles for the Ellen Smith fleet and later transferred to Coachways; then to Rossendale in 2004.

Previously registered WSV 550/3 and originally G900 MNS, G899 MNS, respectively.

ROSSENDALE TRANSPORT LIMITED

Date In	Date Out	Former Operator	Notes
2000	2000	Dawsonrentals (hired)	
2000	2000	Dawsonrentals (hired)	
2000	2005/6	Lothian Buses	Ex B43D
2000	2005	Arriva Midlands North	
2000		new	
2001	2005, 2004	Brighton & Hove	
2001	2003	Ellen Smith	m
2001	2003	Ellen Smith	n
2001		new	
2002		new	
2002		new	
2002		new	
2002		new	
2002		new	
2002		Blue Bus, Bolton	
2003		Blue Bus, Bolton	
2003		Blue Bus, Bolton	
2003		new	o
2003		new	
2003		new	
2003		new	
2003		Volvo Bus, Warwick (demonstrator)	
2003/4		Metrobus	p
2004		new	k
2004		new	k
2004		Coachways	l
2004		new	
2004		new	
2004		new	
2005		new	
2005		new	
2005		new	
2005		2 Travel, Pentrechwyth	
2005		2 Travel, Pentrechwyth	
2005		2 Travel, Pentrechwyth	
2006		Halton Borough Transport	
2006		Halton Borough Transport	
2006		Munro's, JedburghNotes	

Notes continued

m. Purchased from Harrogate & District in 2000 for the Ellen Smith fleet.
n. Purchased from Border, Burnley in 1996 for the Ellen Smith fleet.
o. Exhibited at the Coach & Bus Show, Birmingham, in September 1993.
p. 23 and 24 repainted in Haslingden Corporation and Rawtenstall Corporation livery, respectively to commemorate 100 years of municipal operations.

EST Later transferred to Ellen Smith (Tours) Limited and renumbered.

General

It has not proved possible within the constraints of the publishing deadlines to detail the considerable number of demonstration and other loan or hire vehicles that have been operated or inspected, particularly in the post-1986 period. It is hoped that at some point in the future, this information along with much more detail than the scope of this publication allows, will feature in an extended history of Rossendale Transport and its predecessors.

ROSSENDALE TRANSPORT LIMITED

Vehicle upgrades – new bodywork fitted to refurbished chassis

No.	Registration	Chassis type	Body type and seating	Chassis new	Body New	Date Out
70-71	PJI 9170/1	Leyland PSU4D/2R	East Lancs EL2000 B47F	1977	1993	2003
75	PJI 9175	Leyland PSU3E/4R	East Lancs EL2000 B51F	1980	1993	2002
77	PJI 9177	Leyland PSU3C/4R	East Lancs EL2000 B51F	1977	1992	2003
78	PJI 9178	Leyland PSU3E/4R	East Lancs EL2000 B51F	1979	1992	2002
79	PJI 9179	Leyland PSU3E/4R	East Lancs EL2000 B51F	1980	1992	2003

Notes
Previous registrations: PHB 362/3R, WCK 139V, UGG 369R, WCK 123V, GRF 268V
70, 71 were previously numbered 162, 163.
77 was numbered 310 in the Ellen Smith fleet.

All operated with their original registrations in rebodied form before receiving the PJI series registration marks.

In addition, three more vehicles joined the fleet having been rebodied for their previous operators by East Lancs. They are shown in the main listing above, but were also given registration marks in the same block of numbers used on the 'native' rebodies. Some of these registrations had been used on other vehicles.

No.	Registration	Chassis type	Body type and seating	Chassis new	Body New	Date Out
73	PJI 9173	Volvo B10M-61	East Lancs EL2000 B51F	1981	1992	2003
74	PJI 9174	Leyland TRCTL11/3R	East Lancs EL2000 B53F	1981	1993	2002
76	PJI 9176	Leyland PSU3E/4R	East Lancs EL2000 B51F	1977	1992	2003

Notes

Previous registrations: NCS 117W, BSG 551W, VAJ 784S.
74 was converted into a permanent driver training vehicle in 2002 and was withdrawn in 2005. It is still owned.

Waiting at the Bacup Road timing point opposite the depot in Rawtenstall in August 2006 is Wright-bodied Volvo number 153 *en route* from Accrington to Rochdale. *(HP)*

Facing page: A farewell presentation to Roger Bowker, Managing Director from 1981 to 1984 shows left to right – George Green, Kenneth Howarth, Wendy Burton, Councillor Pickup, Roger Bowker and Tom Swift. *(RT)*

APPENDIX 2

ROSSENDALE TRANSPORT LIMITED
Bus Routes as at 31st August 1982

No.	Route Details	Joint operator/Notes
4	Accrington - Baxenden - Haslingden - Rawtenstall - Bacup	Hyndburn
6	Rawtenstall - Hall Carr	
7	Rawtenstall - Oakley	
8	Rawtenstall - Newchurch - Waterfoot	
9	Waterfoot - Edgeside	
10	Waterfoot - Booth Road - Britannia	
11	Rawtenstall - Gregory Fold - Haslingden	
13	Haslingden - Gregory Fold - Helmshore - Grane Road - Haslingden	
14	Haslingden - Grane Road - Helmshore - Gregory Fold - Haslingden	
15	Rawtenstall - Waterfoot - Cowpe	
16	Rawtenstall - Balladen	
17	Rawtenstall - Rossendale General Hospital	
20	Haslingden - Hud Rake - Rising Bridge Road - Stonefold	
21	Haslingden - Ewood Bridge - Irwell Vale	
32	Bacup - Weir - Deerplay - Towneley - Burnley	Ribble
236	Rawtenstall - Waterfoot - Water - Burnley	Ribble
247	Bacup - Sharneyford	Ribble, W.Yorks PTE
273	Bolton - Bradshaw - Ramsbottom - Edenfield - Rawtenstall - Crawshawbooth - Burnley	Ribble, GMT
473	Bury - Walmersley - Shuttleworth - Edenfield - Rawtenstall - Crawshawbooth - Burnley.	Ribble, GMT.
474	Bury - Holcombe - Ramsbottom - Edenfield - Rawtenstall	Gr. Manchester Trans.
-	Ramsbottom -Haslingden - Rawtenstall - Todmorden	Note 1

Notes

1. Feeder service for Burnley & Pendle service from Colne to London

APPENDIX 3

ROSSENDALE TRANSPORT LIMITED
SERVICES REGISTERED FOR DEREGULATION DAY

REG. REF.	SER.No.	ROUTE DETAILS	OP.DAYS
PC/0599/1838	4	Accrington - Haslingden - Rawtenstall - Bacup	Daily
PC/0595/1838	5	Balladen - Rawtenstall - Water	M-S
PC/0596/1838	6	Rawtenstall - Sharnyford / Weir	M-S
PC/1573/1838	7	Rawtenstall - Waterfoot - Hey Head - Bacup	Wed. Sat.
PC/1561/1838	8	Rawtenstall - Ski Rossendale	M-S
PC/0598/1838	11/12	Rawtenstall - Haslingden - Rawtenstall	M-S
PC/1560/1838	15	Rawtenstall - Waterfoot - Cowpe	M-S
PC/1559/1838	17	Rawtenstall - Rawtenstall General Hospital	M-S
PC/0597/1838	273	Bolton - Rawtenstall - Burnley	M-S
PC/1236/1838	465/466	Bacup - Whitworth - Rochdale	M-S
PC/1238/1838	474	Bury - Stubbins - Rawtenstall	M-S
PC/1239/1838	472	Rawtenstall - Walmersley - Bury	M-S
PC/1237/1838	-	Rawtenstall - Britannia - Bacup - Water	M-F Works Service

In addition to the above 'Local Services' 27 Schools Services were registered

ACKNOWLEDGEMENTS

The author and publisher acknowledge with gratitude the help of many organisations and individuals in the preparation of this book. The staff at Rawtenstall Library were particularly helpful in making available information and photographs whilst the resources of the Omnibus Society and the PSV Circle have, as ever, been invaluable. The management and staff at Rossendale Transport have provided information and encouragement and Barry Drelincourt, Commercial Director, has provided the detailed information used in the chapter on Rossendale Transport Limited, covering the time of expansion and leading to the present position of the Company.

Books on the general history of the area have been consulted including 'Haslingden' by Chris Aspin and Derek Pilkington, also 'Mr Pilling's Short Cut to China' by Chris Aspin published by Helmshore Local History Society, 'Around Ramsbottom' and 'Ramsbottom Reminiscences' published by Ramsbottom Heritage Society. On the transport scene reference has been made to *Buses* magazine and to 'Hyndburn and Rossendale – 75 Years of Municipal Operation' by Peter Deegan and published by the Omnibus Society. The author's neighbours, Norman and Hazel Cunliffe, who originate from the area, have also supplied useful information.

The Parsons family, through Ron and later his widow and children, made available items collected by Ron's father, Sidney, during his position as Manager of the Ramsbottom system from 1920-1951.

John Cronshaw has made available his vast knowledge of the area and the bus operations within it over many years and has compiled the fleet summaries. Ken Swallow, Roy Marshall, and the Omnibus Society have also provided information and Alan Pritchard from the British Commercial Vehicle Museum (BCVM) has been most helpful.

I am especially grateful to David and Mary Shaw who have meticulously checked the proofs and John Hewson who read the text. Any errors are mine and not theirs, however. The author acknowledges the help of John Senior in applying his expertise in putting everything together to create the finished book.

Acknowledgement is also made to the many photographers without whom the book would not have materialised. Where the source of a photograph is known, acknowledgement has been made with the individual photographs using the following key :-

RLIB	Rawtenstall Library	HL	Haslingden Library	RT	Rossendale Transport
RM	Roy Marshall	RMC	Roy Marshall Collection	MB	Mark Bailey
BD	Bob Downham	JC	John Cronshaw	LM	Leyland Motors
CMC	Colin McKernan Collection	PF	The Parsons Family	HP	Author
STA	Senior Transport Archive	JAS	John Senior	DP	David Powell
BCVM	British Commercial Vehicle Museum	MTMS	Manchester Transport Museum Society		

Harry Postlethwaite,
Blackpool,
June 2007